FROM THE
DR. DOUG TIPPIN

A
MAN
AFTER
GOD'S
HEART

1+ - ∅

Discovery House Publishers

Books, music, and videos that feed the soul with the Word of God

Box 3566 Grand Rapids, MI 49501

Luis Palau

A MAN AFTER GOD'S HEART

**RUNNING
WITH DAVID**

Library of Congress Cataloging-in-Publication Data

Palau, Luis, 1934–
    [Heart after God]
    A man after God's heart / by Luis Palau.
    Originally published: Heart after God. Portland, Or. : Multnomah Press,
c1978.
    ISBN 1-57293-030-6
    1. David, King of Israel—Meditations.
BS580.D3P28   1998
248.4—dc21   97-51672
                                                         CIP

98 00 02 03 01 99
CHG
1 3 5 7 9 10 8 6 4 2

Contents

Preface

WHILE STILL A TEENAGER, David was taking long strides toward greatness. His trail, though haunted by loneliness, tragedy, and broken dreams, climbed heights few have scaled since. David ran toward his God. Even today, his life gives birth to dreams. Young men and women who take time to unearth his footprints feel a tug at the feet to follow.

But the teen-age giant killer had giants to face as an adult, too. We read of David the great king, David the leader of nations, but we also read of a man with passions like our own who struggled and failed yet gathered up the broken pieces to give back to God. A man after God; a heart after God's heart.

David's dependence on spiritual resources coupled with his incessant forward action conquered a nation for God's purposes. Now, centuries later, the son of Jesse goes right on conquering lives and hearts for the Lord he loved and served.

David's life speaks with power to this generation. Facing almost impossible moral pressures and relentless assaults on the family, this generation needs to hear that a pattern of victory is possible. Utilizing principles practiced by David can provide us with God-appointed weapons.

A Man After God's Heart

In his triumph or in his failure, the son of Jesse teaches us. The message from David's life for this age is that we too can be men and women after God's own heart.

Someone who has demonstrated his heart for God is Larry Libby. He worked long and hard over this manuscript, not only as a professional but also with deep devotion of heart to our Lord Jesus Christ. My thanks also to Jeanne Doering, who assisted Larry in this project, and to Kim Claassen, who did so much to make this new Discovery House edition a reality. I thank God that we are "fellow workers" with Christ (2 Corinthians 6:1).

And now, may God be pleased to demonstrate through the life of this young king of Israel what He can do today through you. May He so mold your life that you will have a heart that beats in rhythm with His own.

—Luis Palau
Acts 13:22

Chapter 1

Where Kings Part Company

THE CHOICES WE MAKE determine the shape and color of our lives.

It doesn't work that way very often. Many of life's most crucial decisions occur in lonely, open fields where you can't even find rabbit tracks. Others are made in congested thoroughfares where it's so crowded your feet don't even touch the pavement as you move with the throng at the pedestrian crossing. Some decisions are far enough down the road that you have plenty of time to think about them before the road forks. Other decisions open suddenly at your feet, demanding instant action.

At such moments as these, when crisis flashes from a clear sky, *what* you know isn't as important as *who* you know. The important question to ask is not so much, "Am I walking in the right direction?" but rather, "Am I walking with the Director?" If you've been walking daily with the living God, drawing your life from Him, the crisis step is simply the next step.

"Here I am, Lord—instant decision time. You know that I want Your best in this so lead on! I'll be right behind."

If, on the other hand, you're walking in dependence on yourself—your own judgment—the crisis step can be terrifying. One wrong turn can alter a lifetime.

Two men, Saul and David, approached the same intersection together and parted company. One man ascended the stairs to unparalleled honor while the other fell broken and disgraced into the basement of obscurity.

The two of them had the same privileges, the same opportunities, the same background, and the same brilliant blessings of God. Yet only one of them found favor in the annals of Israel. Today the Star of *David* flutters proudly over the King *David* Hotel in Jerusalem. Think of it! After thirty centuries the name of David is esteemed all over the world, while Saul, Israel's first king, is somewhere back in the dim shadows.

Choices! All through life we approach critical, irreversible decisions. Only a few, momentary choices spelled the difference between the destiny of a Saul and the destiny of a David. It wasn't their environment. It wasn't their parents or their education that separated their paths. It was the choices they made in the instant of crisis. And when you get down to the bottom line, making choices is making the difference in your life, too.

ANOINTED AND APPOINTED

Both Saul and David felt the anointing oil of Samuel the prophet splash through their curls and trickle onto their broad shoulders while they were still young men.

Regarding Saul, Scripture says:

> *Now the day before Saul came, the LORD had revealed this to Samuel: "About this time tomorrow I will send you a man from the land of Benjamin. Anoint him leader over my people Israel; he will deliver my people from the hand of the Philistines. I have looked upon my people, for their cry has reached me."*
>
> *When Samuel caught sight of Saul, the LORD said to him, "This is the man I spoke to you about; he will govern my people"* (1 Samuel 9:15–17).

Saul never sought the position of king. In that respect, he was like King George VI of England, and the American presidents Lyndon Johnson and Gerald Ford. Johnson acquired the office because of assassination. Ford, through resignation. George VI, through abdication. Saul was anointed, which means he was appointed! God chose Saul and said, "Saul shall be king in Israel."

David was God-appointed, too. The same prophet who poured the oil on Saul was sent out with another bottle to a Bethlehem address. At the right moment, God said to Samuel:

> *"How long will you mourn for Saul, since I have rejected him as king over Israel? Fill your horn with oil and be on your way; I am sending*

11

you to Jesse of Bethlehem. I have chosen one of his sons to be king" (1 Samuel 16:1).

So the prophet visited Jesse and asked to see his sons. Seven of them filed past, one by one, as Samuel fingered his flowing gray beard. I can see old Samuel piercing the Bethlehemite with a steely stare from under his great, bushy eyebrows.

"Are you sure this is *all* of them?" the prophet rumbled.

"Well . . . all of them? Um . . . well . . . almost all of them . . . I mean . . . that is to say . . . not exactly all of them . . . there is one more out in the pasture—a mere child you understand—looking after a few sheep. But you wouldn't . . . that is, he couldn't . . . er . . . ah . . . we shouldn't . . . .

"Bring him in!"

So he sent and had him brought in. He was ruddy, with a fine appearance and handsome features.

Then the LORD said, "Rise and anoint him; he is the one" (1 Samuel 16:12).

BORN AGAIN

Not only were both Saul and David anointed, both of them also had a new-birth experience. Many people ask me, "Do you really think that Saul was 'born again'?" I answer *yes*. Even though his life ended in a tragic tangle of knots, the Scripture indicates that Saul had the Old Testament equivalent of a second-birth experience.

Back a few chapters in 1 Samuel 10, Saul had an encounter with some prophets right after he was anointed.

Samuel had said this would happen to verify that God had chosen the young Benjamite. Sketching verses 5–10:

> *"Afterward you will go to Gibeah of God . . .*
> *and you will be changed into a different person"*
> *. . . God changed Saul's heart . . . the Spirit of God*
> *came upon him.*

Doesn't that mean Saul was born again? If God gives you a new heart and the Holy Spirit comes upon you, what more do you want? If that isn't being reborn, I don't know what is.

We know David was reborn because the Lord says of him, "I have found in David the son of Jesse a man after my heart, who will do all my will" (Acts 13:22). Being in harmony with God's own heart usually indicates that a person has been born again.

ALL OF THIS AND GOOD LOOKS, TOO

Third, both men enjoyed great physical advantages. In 1 Samuel 9:2, we read about Saul whom the Scripture portrays as:

> *. . . an impressive young man without equal among*
> *the Israelites—a head taller than any of the others.*

The son of Kish was a head-turner. Hollywood material. Towering head and shoulders above the crowd, he would have had pro basketball scouts lined up outside his door if he were around today. He had all the qualities, humanly speaking, that most of us look for in a leader.

A Man After God's Heart

"Now *there's* a leader," people will say. "Look how tall he is. And how about that mustache!" It doesn't always follow, but many people feel this way and the people of Israel were no exception.

A few years later we see David. Slightly younger than Saul at the time of his anointing, David's portrait is sketched in Scripture like this:

> *Now he was ruddy, and had beautiful eyes,*
> *and was handsome* (1 Samuel 16:12, RSV).

"Ruddy" simply means sun-tanned. He had a healthy look to him. But there was something special about the sun-tan David wore. In fact, there was something special for everybody in David's looks. He was bronzed and brown so his mama thought he was good-looking, had beautiful eyes so the girls thought he was good-looking, and was handsome so even the men had to admit he was good-looking.

And, like Saul, this well-favored specimen was also filled with God's Holy Spirit from his youth.

HIDING IN THE BAGGAGE

Despite all their privileges, each of these men began their stellar careers with a truly humble attitude. Even as teenagers they weren't arrogant, pushy, or stomping all over other people.

Saul was so humble he almost missed his own coronation day. The people had gathered from all over Israel to see the big Benjamite crowned king. The bands were playing and the flags were flying. But there was one person missing—Saul! Nobody could find him. Finally, someone

14

spotted his large frame only half-hidden behind a trunk and a suitbag in the back corner of a baggage room. Instead of strutting around signing autographs and kissing babies as any sensible politician would have done in a crowd like that, the intended king was trying to stay out of sight. Why was he hiding? Because he had a humble attitude. Even though he was handsome, spiritually reborn, and divinely appointed to the throne, Saul felt unworthy and undeserving. He kept hoping it would all blow over so he could ride back to his dad's ranch in Benjamite country.

And when a bunch of "worthless fellows" mocked him and ridiculed his inauguration, Saul refused to retaliate.

"You think *he's* going to deliver us?" they jeered. "Ah, we're not going to give him anything but a hard time." Saul wasn't blind or thickheaded. He saw it and heard it. And he let it go. The Bible says he absolutely ignored them and kept silent.

We find the same attitude in David. Saul's effort to persuade the son of Jesse to marry one of his daughters is told in 1 Samuel 18. You'd think David would leap at the chance. To marry the king's daughter would mean privilege, position, and special opportunities by the score.

But look at the passage:

> *Then Saul ordered his attendants: "Speak to David privately and say, 'Look, the king is pleased with you, and his attendants all like you; now become his son-in-law.'"*
>
> *They repeated these words to David. But David said, "Do you think it is a small matter to become*

*the king's son-in-law? I am only a poor man and
little known"* (1 Samuel 18:22–23).

Even though he had known since his anointing when
he was a teenager that he would someday be king, his heart
remained humble.

They were all saying, "Come on, David. We all love
you. The king wants you in the family. And have you seen
his daughter? You're foolish if you pass this up. You've got
everything to gain and nothing to lose. Now how about it?"

"It's no small thing to marry the king's daughter,"
David replied. "Me? Marry into the royal family? You've
got to be joking. Who am I? I'm just a shepherd and a poor
shepherd at that."

David knew he was going to be king. And he was popular—the talk of all Israel. He'd beaten Goliath with a single stone and ballads on his bravery were topping the charts
from Dan to Beersheba. Yet because of his humility, David
turned down Saul's initial offer to become a son-in-law.

WHAT'S THE DIFFERENCE?

The hand of God rested on both men in a clear and
unusual way. Both young kings were valiant generals and
succeeded in beating and battering the enemies of Israel in
battle after battle. Both were crowned near the same age.
Both were husbands. Both were fathers.

What tremendous young men they were! Privileged
and blessed of God in every way. So you say to yourself,
"What's the difference? Why do we remember David as a
great man and Saul as a defeated man? The name of David

echoes through Scripture with splendor and power . . .
through the Prophets . . . the Gospels . . . the Epistles . . . the
Apocalypse . . . But Saul? It's like someone padlocked the
file. What happened?"

All of us know people who had everything going for
them, people who started out strong. Loaded with talent,
enthusiasm, and personality, their lives seemed to radiate
potential for Christ. Everything was in their favor. Things
were going great. Then suddenly—they drop out of sight.
Talk floats back of a marriage breakup. Something happened that nobody wants to talk about because it's so
embarrassing. And you wonder, what happened? What happened to Joe? Where's Mary these days? What happened?

Today is no different from the days of Saul and David.
People are confronted by choices. Lives hinge on decisions
forged in the heat of crisis. Some lives break loose from the
moorings of mediocrity and sail new seas for the honor of
Christ. Other lives bog down on sandbars and never make it
out of the harbor.

With a couple of tragic exceptions, David made the
right decisions at the right time. When a crisis rolled in like
a sudden typhoon, he was ready. He didn't need to panic and
start thumbing madly through the phone book for God's
number. He had it memorized a long time before. Out in the
hills of Judah, alone with his sheep through the long nights,
he dialed it frequently—and never found a busy signal. You
can find many of their intimate conversations recorded in a
book called *Psalms*.

Saul, slipping into the snare of self-reliance, carelessly
left the phone off the hook. He didn't listen carefully to

God's instructions. By the time the emergency was on top of the foolish king, it was too late.

How is it with your answering service? Disconnected? Maybe you've put God on "hold" and left Him there for years. Better clear the lines. There might be an emergency call waiting.

A Kingdom Canceled, a Kingdom Confirmed

IT COMES TO OUR DOOR in a variety of costumes, introducing itself by a number of different names. Broken relationships. Infertility. Miscarriage. Business failure. Downsizing. Daughter on drugs. Son with AIDS. Separation. Divorce. Cancer. Death of a loved one. When crisis comes—and it always comes—how do you meet it?

Most of us live like normal, regular Smith-and-Jones kinds of people until crisis hurtles in and shatters our routine. People can learn a great deal about you by watching how you react in a moment of crisis. All the outward window dressing is jerked aside, revealing the reality of your walk with God. What are people learning about the sufficiency of Jesus Christ from observing your responses under sudden pressure?

When things are going smoothly, most of us can swing it. We can quote verses, sing hymns, show up at church, and stay more or less in tune. But when an emergency washes across our tranquil landscape—what then?

The late Ray Stedman, under whom Charles Swindoll and I served as pastoral interns years ago at Peninsula Bible Church in Palo Alto, California, used to say, "Woe to the man who has to learn principles at a time of crisis." He should be learning those truths *before* the walls collapse. Otherwise, he'll be confused, overwhelmed, and constantly bullied around by his circumstances. His first reaction may be a long and bitter complaint directed against God.

"Oh, Lord . . . how could you allow this to happen? How does a God of love permit this? I've been faithful to the church. I've given my money to the carpet fund. If God can't help me now—I'm quitting! If this is the way God pays me . . . ."

Suddenly Mr. Pillar-of-the-Church begins to sound just like his pagan neighbor. It happens all too often. Usually in the heat of crisis. At that point, at that decisive instant, a choice must be made. How we choose to respond at that crossroads could either pump fresh faith into our spiritual veins or set us back ten years in our witness and our walk with God.

Do you find yourself blaming God when the furnace of affliction begins to heat up? Saul did. When the pressure was on, we find Saul immediately acting as if he'd never known the Lord.

What a difference, though, with David. When he was persecuted, rather than blaming the Lord, David would say, "Well, the Lord knows I deserve to be persecuted." When he had to hide, he would say, "The Lord knows why I have to hide." He related every event in his life to the hand of the Lord.

The fall of Saul cannot be traced to one awful, dramatic, disastrous, instantaneous failure. Few people ever fail that way. With Saul, a series of wrong turns brought his life and his kingdom to ruin. Wrong choice after wrong choice. Wrong response after wrong response. Missing the right turn at one crucial intersection, Saul would panic and take one wrong turn after another. Instead of going back to the place where he first lost his direction, he kept getting in deeper.

Let's try to trace his route. We know his eventual destination: failure, folly, suicide. But how did he end up at a place like that? How did a man with such a brilliant future end up in such a dark and hopeless back alley?

Wrong Turn No. 1: Impatience

One of Saul's most damaging dead-end routes bore a road sign reading: "Impatience." Look at 1 Samuel 13. Saul and his men were preparing for war against the Philistine army, which had the Israelite camp surrounded. Tension was high, and Saul was eager to attack. Then, just when everything seemed ripe to launch an offensive, Samuel the prophet left for seven days. It was time for the sacrifice to be offered before battle, but Samuel was out of town.

Before he departed, the old prophet left the king with a firm directive. "Wait until I return," Samuel told him. "When

A Man After God's Heart

I get back in seven days, we'll offer a sacrifice to the Lord and after that we'll go to war. Then the Lord will give us the victory."

Day one passed. Everyone was getting nervous. Captains of the troops kept riding in to report that the soldiers' morale was ebbing and couldn't something be done soon? Day two. Day three. Day four. The enemy was only on the other side of the hill and the anticipation had everyone itchy. You could cut the tension in camp with a knife. Even the mules were restless. Still no Samuel. Day six. Some of the people began to walk out on Saul, heading back home. In the meantime, the king was becoming feverishly impatient.

"Where is that old man? What kind of time is this to take a holiday?"

Day seven.

Piling wood on the altar, Saul decided to "get things ready" for Samuel. Daylight revealed that still more soldiers had deserted the Israelite cause. The sun climbed higher in the sky and still the prophet tarried.

Finally Saul could stand it no longer. Maybe something had happened to the old man. He *had* to get the troops out and fighting. Wasn't that a king's responsibility? So even though Samuel was the only one who was supposed to offer sacrifices, Saul said:

> *"Bring me the burnt offering and the fellowship offerings." And Saul offered up the burnt offering* (1 Samuel 13:9).

Just as he was finishing, Samuel came striding into camp. Saul hurried to meet him.

22

A Kingdom Canceled, a Kingdom Confirmed

"What have you done?" Samuel asked.

Listen how Saul tried to justify his actions.

> *"When I saw that the men were scattering, and that you did not come at the set time, and that the Philistines were assembling at Micmash, I thought, 'Now the Philistines will come down against me at Gilgal, and I have not sought the LORD's favor.' So I felt compelled to offer the burnt offering"* (1 Samuel 13:11–12).

Samuel wasn't one to waste time on niceties. He called the king of Israel a fool.

> *"You acted foolishly. You have not kept the command the LORD your God gave you; if you had, he would have established your kingdom over Israel for all time. But now your kingdom will not endure; the LORD has sought out a man after his own heart and appointed him leader of his people, because you have not kept the LORD's command"* (1 Samuel 13:13–14).

Having delivered Saul this devastating blow, the old prophet wheeled around and walked out of camp, leaving the king standing open-mouthed before the smoldering altar.

You and I might say that what Saul did wasn't so bad. It was just a simple matter of rushing ahead of the Lord *a little*, right? The enemy armies were surrounding him. The seventh day had come and the prophet hadn't shown. So what do you do? Saul simply took matters into his own hands and kindled the sacrifice on his own.

A Man After God's Heart

Impatience. How many of us have ruined rare and unusual opportunities to serve Christ because of impatience? It doesn't seem like such a big thing and yet—do you know what impatience represents? It is a sign of distrust in the sovereign control of God. We demonstrate by our hasty actions that we really don't believe our God is in loving control of every event entering our lives. Impatience, then, is another word for *unbelief.*

We jump the gun and insist on beating the Lord to the draw. Somehow we become convinced that our God has lost control of the circumstances in our lives. Or that He really doesn't care.

"My soul," we say, "the whole thing's falling apart! I'm going to have to intervene in this myself. If the Lord can't handle it, well, I surely can. I've been to college. I've had experience. Let me at it."

Through the years, my wife and I have seen a number of couples and families become ensnared in this trap called impatience. I think of one young couple in particular. The Lord seemed to be opening doors for them, using their lives in a clear and visible way. Then they got impatient. It wasn't happening fast enough for them. They wanted to move on. Their pastor saw some serious problems with their proposed move and advised them, "Don't go." We were their friends, and one night we were at their home for dinner. As they asked for counsel, we told them, "Don't go." Many other people in the church also said, "Don't go. Don't go."

But no. "God was leading." They just wouldn't wait. Against all advice, they packed up and moved.

What happened? It wasn't long before things began to fall apart. The man lost his job. The woman became confused and unhappy. They began to fight and lost all chance of ministry. Why? They were simply too impatient to wait for the Lord's time. Those who loved them counseled them to wait. All the circumstances said, "Hang in there. Wait for the Lord's best time." But they had to jump right in.

Refusing to wait for God's green light, King Saul leaped straight into disaster. Impatience is no joke. Unbelief is a grief to the heart of God. Apart from the empowering presence of the indwelling Christ, this sin of impatience could be *my* downfall. Or yours. For Saul, it was the first wrong turn leading directly to another one.

WRONG TURN NO. 2: PARTIAL OBEDIENCE

Wheeling down the road of impatience, Saul easily merged onto the broad highway of disobedience.

Back on the battlefield again, the king was preparing to make a strike against Israel's long-time adversary, the Amalekites. God had said, "The Amalekites are my enemies. I want them totally destroyed—every living thing. They refused to help the children of Israel as they came out of Egypt. And now, these many years later, they are totally corrupt. Let nothing live—wipe out everything." The instructions were clear.

So Saul and his armies marched on the Amalekites and destroyed them . . . almost. They demolished everything . . . except . . . they did not kill the king, they saved the best of the livestock, and they kept a few good things like gold and treasures. The rest—the junk of the land—they dutifully burned and destroyed. So the smoke billowed from the villages of the Amalekites, but the Israelites marched out with a few little goodies because they figured these were too nice and too good. And besides, you wouldn't want to kill a king.

Was God pleased with this "interpretation" of His command? Look at the record:

> *Then the word of the LORD came to Samuel: "I am grieved that I have made Saul king, because he has turned away from me, and has not carried out my instructions." Samuel was troubled, and he cried to the LORD all that night.*
>
> *Early in the morning Samuel got up and went to meet Saul, but was told, "Saul has gone to Carmel. There he has set up a monument in his own honor and has turned and gone on down to Gilgal."*
>
> *When Samuel reached him, Saul said, "The LORD bless you! I have carried out the LORD's instructions."*
>
> *But Samuel said, "What then is this bleating of the sheep in my ears? What is this lowing of cattle that I hear?"* (1 Samuel 15:10–14).

You'll notice that Saul's actions weren't *total* disobedience. It wasn't as if he had said, "Look Samuel. I just don't have the heart to kill these Amalekites. No sir. That's a nasty little job—too much bloodshed. I will not do it." No, he didn't say that.

He did what he was told—with just a few exceptions. It wasn't out-and-out insubordination. It was partial obedience. He didn't carry out the full instructions.

A Kingdom Canceled, a Kingdom Confirmed

In the same way, it usually isn't gross sin or blatant immorality that sinks many Christians. It is "almost obedience." Notice that God did not take Saul's partial obedience lightly. "What you have done is rebellion!" he said through Samuel.

Rebellion? Isn't that a little strong? That's what Saul thought.

"*Who* rebelled? Not me, Samuel. I went on the mission. I killed the Amalekites. The whole place is in flames. So we kept a few sheep and cows and didn't kill the king. Is that such a big thing?"

But the Lord had said, "Do it all." It wasn't up to Saul to decide what he was going to do and what he wasn't going to do. The Lord hadn't asked for evaluation or interpretation. He asked for obedience.

> Samuel said, "Although you were once small in your own eyes, did you not become the head of the tribes of Israel? The LORD anointed you king over Israel. And he sent you on a mission, saying, 'Go and completely destroy those wicked people, the Amalekites; make war on them until you have wiped them out.' Why then did you not obey the LORD? Why did you pounce on the plunder and do evil in the eyes of the LORD?" (1 Samuel 15:17–19).

There must have been sorrow in the prophet's voice as he confronted the disobedient king. Samuel's sorrow and God's sorrow.

"Oh Saul, son of Kish, the Lord chose you, singled you out from among all the tribes of Israel. Though you were small and unimportant in your own sight the God of your fathers selected you for unprecedented blessing. He poured out honor and privilege and favor upon you even as I poured the anointing oil over your head. But more than that, He poured Himself into your life. He gave you His own Spirit as Companion, Guide, and never-failing Fountain of strength. How then could you turn your back on all that to satisfy your own selfish desires?"

Saul adapted God's Word to suit his own agenda. He rearranged it to fit his own lifestyle, doing such a clever job that he almost fooled himself.

"Wait a minute!" he cried. "I *did* obey the Lord. I wiped out those Amalekites. See—here is their king and here are their best animals which we want to sacrifice to the Lord."

> *But Samuel replied,*
> *"Does the LORD delight in burnt offerings*
> *and sacrifices*
> *as much as in obeying the voice of the LORD?*
> *To obey is better than sacrifice,*
> *and to heed is better than the fat of rams.*
> *For rebellion is like the sin of divination,*
> *and arrogance is like the evil of idolatry.*
> *Because you have rejected the word of the LORD,*
> *he has rejected you as king"*
> (1 Samuel 15:22–23).

It's the same with us. God isn't interested in our fanfare and flashy spiritual speeches. What He wants is our simple obedience. All the way—from the heart.

A Kingdom Canceled, a Kingdom Confirmed

As our evangelistic team travels worldwide, we've seen it in the lives of many, many believers. Partial obedience. Maybe you break with some sinful things you don't like anyway. But you hang onto a few selected goodies. You say, "Well, let's not be extremists. Surely a little is all right." Of course, you wouldn't do too much. Just a little playing around. "No, I wouldn't be caught in a strip joint, but looking at a little light pornography on the Internet isn't going to hurt anybody. It's just a few pictures. And watching this questionable cable TV program isn't that bad. You have to know how the world thinks, don't you? It's not like you're going all out . . . ."

So you give an inch here, a foot there, and before you know it you're out of the race. You've lost the power, you've lost the anointing.

Although Saul continued to be king in the technical sense, in reality his kingdom was canceled. From then on nobody paid much attention to him. People knew he was finished. Even his own son said, "My dad doesn't have it anymore." Having drifted so far from God's chosen course, Saul burned out and dead-ended on the back road . . . the wrong roads.

"Rebellion," says the Scripture, "is as the sin of divination, and arrogance like the evil of idolatry." (1 Samuel 15:23) In other words, in God's sight, rebellion is like going into the occult. We shake our heads when we read about someone dabbling in the occult, don't we? And we say, "Oh, the occult, uh—oh . . . ." Of course, we ought to be afraid of the occult. But God says when we rebel—that is, when knowingly we partially obey—that is the same as consorting with demons.

And then He says, "Arrogance [is] like the evil of idolatry." We may be horrified to see someone praying to a statue of a saint. Or shocked to see some savage bowing to the sun and the moon. But the Bible says arrogance before God is the same as falling on your face before Buddha. Has the Lord been speaking to you about a particular area of your life? Be careful if you are considering the route of stubborn resistance.

WRONG TURN NO. 3: OATHS, THREATS, AND CURSES

By the time we arrive in 1 Samuel 14, all the phone lines between Saul and his God have been severed. The Holy Spirit has removed His hand of blessing from the unhappy king. The wrong turns come easier now—with increasing frequency.

The scene opens in the midst of another battle with the Philistines. Relying on his own strength and wisdom—out of touch with God—Saul made a foolish oath:

> *Now the men of Israel were in distress that day, because Saul had bound the people under an oath, saying, "Cursed be any man who eats food before evening comes, before I have avenged myself on my enemies!" So none of the troops tasted food* (1 Samuel 14:24).

Saul's son, Jonathan, hadn't heard about the curse. As the battle stretched on through the day, a number of the Israelites passed through a forest where honeycomb was in abundance. Exhausted and famished, Jonathan speared a piece with the end of his staff and chewed on it as the troops maneuvered through the trees. The effect of the honey was instantaneous. Verse 27 says, "He raised his hand to his mouth, and his eyes brightened."

It must have been obvious. Among the bone-weary, half-starved soldiers of Israel, Jonathan's bright eyes shone like beacons.

> *Then one of the soldiers told him, "Your father bound the army under a strict oath, saying, 'Cursed be any man who eats food today!' That is why the men are faint."*
>
> *Jonathan said, "My father has made trouble for the country. See how my eyes brightened when I tasted a little of this honey. How much better it would have been if the men had eaten today some of the plunder they took from their enemies. Would not the slaughter of the Philistines have been even greater?"* (1 Samuel 14:28–30).

That very evening Saul was ready to execute his own son for violating his foolish, arbitrary oath against eating. At that point, however, the citizen soldiers of Israel mounted an overwhelming protest against the actions of their king and rescued Jonathan from the murderous intentions of his father.

"You're not going to touch a hair of this young man's head!" they told Saul. And that was that. But if the people hadn't saved the young prince, King Saul would have run him through with a sword.

What a weird thing to do. While Jonathan was fighting his heart out, claiming the strength of God to scatter the enemy, Saul was dreaming up oaths and curses God never demanded. Saul thought he was acting spiritual, but he was only acting. He was completely out of touch with God, and all his "holy" oaths and regulations were a sham and a show.

I know of parents who think they are being ultraspiritual with their regulations when actually they are miles away from God and His Word. One day at a place in California where I was speaking, a young woman about nineteen years old came for counsel. She was from a Christian family. But her face was troubled.

"Mr. Palau, there's a lot of tension in our home. In a few days my older sister, who is only twenty, is going to pack up and leave. She really can't afford to but she's leaving anyway."

"Why?" I asked.

"Well," she said, "my dad puts restrictions on us that are ridiculous. We don't have big shouting matches, but my sister can't take him any more."

"Give me an example," I said.

"Well, ever since he went to a Christian seminar where he was taught that the father is over the daughter, he has come on so strong that we're hardly allowed to breathe without consulting him. I mean, we even have to ask his permission to go buy a hamburger, and we're nineteen and twenty.

"My sister has a nice Christian boyfriend from our church. But Dad said that whenever she wants to see him they always have to stay where he can see them both—at all times. He told them, 'I don't want you going for a walk behind my back.' My sister says, 'Dad, we're not going to be doing anything wrong. We just want to *talk*.' But Dad says, "The Scripture says to obey your father. Now you stay where I can see you.' "

I couldn't believe it. That kind of oath—that sort of restriction—is unreasonable. Proverbs 26:2 says that an undeserved curse does not come to rest. You can take Scripture and twist it around to bolster your own ego—making it say things that God never intended. That's what this girl's father did and that's what Saul did.

Saul had drifted so far from the mind and heart of God that he was making absurd, pointless rulings to massage his own ego. "I'm the king!" he said. "I have a right. Everybody should submit to my chain of command. Whoever touches any food today—he's finished. He is under a curse." So nobody ate. And Israel could have lost the war.

WRONG TURN NO. 4: "A MONUMENT TO MYSELF"

Notice Saul built for himself a self-exalting monument. Look at 1 Samuel 15:12:

> *Early in the morning Samuel got up and went to meet Saul, but he was told, "Saul has gone to Carmel. There he has set up a monument in his own honor and has turned and gone on down to Gilgal."*

What a contrast to David. Do you know what David lived for all his life? To build a monument. But it wasn't one for himself. Remember what it was? The temple. In all his life so far, David had never made money for himself. He had never grabbed for riches nor appropriated anything. His

33

one big dream in life was to build a temple for the Ark of the Lord. He would lie awake at night and think about it. It was his deepest-felt desire. But what was Saul's desire? To build a monument for himself.

What kind of monument are you building? What will your children see when you've made your exit from the scene? A monument to yourself? A self-serving life that catered to your own desires and your own ego? The landscape is dotted with those sorts of monuments. But you have to watch them closely—they crumble quickly. Other monuments can be erected in your life—monuments that will continue to bring honor to the name of God's Son throughout eternity. I ask you again: What kind of monument are you building?

WRONG TURN NO. 5: DISLOYALTY

As the wick on King Saul's reign burned lower and lower, even his loyalty to loved ones began to flicker and fade. He was disloyal to his son Jonathan as well as to his friend, protector, and best soldier—David. We've already seen 1 Samuel 14:39, where Saul said:

> *"As surely as the LORD who rescues Israel lives, even if it lies with my son Jonathan, he must die."*

As if he were making some statement of grand dedication to God! Saul was a bitter, defeated man sputtering a silly, useless curse. On his own son! That demonstrates the degree to which Saul was disloyal to his own family. No compassion—no mercy. All he wanted was his own way, to somehow reestablish himself in the eyes of the people. But everyone saw through that bit of self-serving hypocrisy!

Remember how many times David fought for Saul, demonstrating kindness and loyalty to the king? (even though he knew Saul was on the way out). Yet Saul was so envious of David that he tried to murder him. Friendship was expendable. Loyalty was expendable. Family ties were expendable. Anything to stay on top of the pile. Anything to defend the ego and look good in the eyes of other people. By the time a man has reached that length of rutted road, it becomes extremely difficult to turn back. The bridges are burned behind. It's almost too late. Almost. Fortunately, the truth about God found in Jeremiah 32:27 is as true today as when God said it:

> *"I am the LORD, the God of all mankind. Is anything too hard for me?"*

WRONG TURN NO. 6: JEALOUSY

One small seed of jealousy, once it takes root in the soil of the soul, can sprout overnight into a sprawling vine of envy. The choking tendrils of jealousy can curl into every area of life, spreading poison and inflammation as it grows. In the latter days of his kingdom, you could hardly recognize the original Saul. He was tied tightly in the vines of envy and revenge.

The beginnings of this cancerous weed in Saul's heart are traced in 1 Samuel 18:5–9. The Scripture states that whenever David went to fight, he was successful. When the young warrior returned from upending the Philistine champion, women from across Israel came out singing, dancing, and playing musical instruments. Their song?

Saul has slain his thousands,
*   and David his tens of thousands . . .*
(1 Samuel 18:7).

The tune was an immediate hit. Young girls sang it in the streets. Soldiers whistled it in formation. Housewives hummed it washing their clothes in the river. Every time Saul heard the song, it was like smoke in his eyes and sand in his teeth.

Saul was very angry; this refrain galled him. "They have credited David with tens of thousands," he thought, "but me with only thousands. What more can he get but the kingdom?" And from that time on Saul kept a jealous eye on David (1 Samuel 18:8–9).

Hatred and jealousy welled up inside the suspicious king. His mind worked constantly, thinking of ways to destroy the young man who was gaining such high regard among the people. Jealousy can often lead a person to try to destroy another's life. We must watch out and weed out the first growth of this damaging weed in our own lives.

I'm an evangelist, and the Lord has blessed my work. We've seen many hundreds of thousands come to Christ. We've preached to many millions. But I really have to watch my heart when I read in a magazine or newspaper about some other young evangelist who is being used in a mighty way by the Lord. Now what is it to me if some Asian evangelist has a big evangelistic crusade? Yet, in my heart, sometimes it's a tremendous temptation to begin to demean this servant of the Lord whom I've never met, simply because he is successful.

I have no problem with Billy Graham, because he's obviously bigger. And my evangelistic team and I are committed to doing all we can to help new, up-and-coming evangelists here in America. We've also been used of God to encourage and equip a number of evangelists elsewhere all around the world. But when someone fills my ears with spectacular reports about some new "Third World" preacher and all he's doing—without our help—it becomes difficult.

"Did you hear about this guy in Africa?" someone will say. "They say he's seen a million people saved in the last ten years." When I hear something like that I have a tendency to wince, thinking, "Come on now. It can't be a million people." I really have to watch it so that this monster of jealousy doesn't start working on me. I have to take it to the Lord Jesus and say, "Oh God, forgive me. After all these years of knowing better, I still have this thing creep up on me."

You may not be an evangelist and so you say, "That's not my problem." But perhaps jealousy sneaks into your life by a different door. Maybe some girl you know is sharper than you and you know it and there's no way you can get around it. She's slim—eats all she wants and never gets fat—and you put on weight eating lettuce and drinking weak tea.

So you find yourself thinking, "I *know* she has a problem. Maybe she doesn't take care of her children." Then you find out that this sharp, slim lady keeps a good house, has happy, well-behaved kids, and also teaches at a junior college twice a week. Your mind keeps working and working. You say to yourself, "It just can't be. She must have a major failing somewhere. Maybe she and her husband don't get along."

Jealousy begins to filter through your pores as you try harder and harder to find fault with the other person and, in effect, murder her. Not with a gun or a knife. But with words—the venomous fruit of the envy vine. At least in your mind you can slay that other individual.

What a destructive force, this jealousy. Like the son of Kish, many Christians have found their life potential for Jesus Christ blighted or blotted out because they gave the treacherous voice of jealousy a hearing in their souls. Don't let it speak! Stop it before you utter the first vile word. Perhaps in the silence that follows you'll be able to discern the still, small voice of the One who loves you— just as you are.

THE BEAUTY OF BROKENNESS

Is it really so surprising that Saul was tempted with impatience, disobedience, making oaths, pride, disloyalty, and jealousy? I don't think so. I have the same temptations. Maybe you have a few. David experienced them, too. But David kept going up while Saul kept going down. Why? Do you know the real difference between Saul and David? It's simple. Never in Saul's life do you find him humbling himself and confessing that he had sinned against the Lord—and really meaning it.

A Kingdom Canceled, a Kingdom Confirmed

One time there was a confession. Samuel said to Saul, "I'm going to leave you." Saul grabbed the prophet's coat and said, "I have sinned. But please come and honor me before the people." It was a fake confession. He only said it to pacify the prophet. What he really wanted was his honor back. He wasn't repenting. He wasn't broken before God. He wasn't confessing his sin. Saul couldn't stand to be humiliated in the eyes of the people. He would have confessed anything to Samuel to salvage his ego.

When the finger of guilt pointed at the deserving king, he usually found ways to dodge or tip it in another direction. He never broke down. Every time, he accused other people. He found excuses.

"Sure hated to take matters in my own hands and offer that sacrifice, but the people, Samuel, those disloyal soldiers of mine, were deserting! What's a king to do? Besides that—hate to remind you, Samuel—you kept delaying and delaying your promised return. A day or two I could see, but a *week*, Samuel? What choice did I have? Unhappy me—I had to force myself to perform your duties . . . . What's that, Samuel? You hear bleating sheep and lowing oxen? It must be these special, pick-of-the-flock animals I brought along for sacrifices. I saw all that fine livestock and thought to myself, 'Saul, that is fine livestock. It would be a shame to waste it when we could sacrifice it to the Lord.' So we herded them all the way here—ready for the altar. Yes sir, we went to a lot of trouble but—no sacrifice is too great. Right, Samuel? Samuel? . . . ."

Shifting the blame is as old as Adam, who blamed Eve, or Eve, who in turn blamed the serpent. Pause for a moment to consider your own life. Could it be you've sensed a real spiritual decline in the last few years? Perhaps your family has been going through a time of stormy tension and instead of saying, "I am to blame," you keep dodging around, pointing at someone else. "It's my wife," you say, "if only she were different." Or, "It's that mother-in-law of mine, these rebellious kids, that uncaring pastor, that cold, lifeless church . . ." and on and on. Anybody but yourself. That was Saul's stumbling block. You rarely find him confessing, "I have sinned against the Lord." You never find him broken.

David, God's man, committed some sins that were actually more terrible than anything Saul had done. But whenever a prophet or someone else confronted him and said, "David, you've done it, man," David would crumble. Falling on his face he would cry, "I've sinned against my God! Oh Lord, have mercy on this sinner." And he would mean it to the depth of his soul. He would confess it all and strive to make it right with God. Then the Lord would say, "All right. You've repented. You've broken. You've confessed. You're forgiven. David, keep going."

"David is a man after my own heart," God would say. But he couldn't say the same about Saul. The ultimate, irreparable decision for Saul was that he was not broken, not repentant, and therefore not forgiven. The Lord gave him chance after chance to change, to turn around. Again and again He sent Samuel. But proud Saul could not admit defeat, or failure, or sin. "I'll tough it out," he thought. "I'll weather the storm and come out of this somehow." He didn't make it.

Which are you—a Saul or a David? Are you a Saul, king and top man on the outside—but dead in your heart, dead in your soul? Or are you a David, willing to accept a slip in public image, willing to be marred in men's eyes if only to be right with God?

If you want to be a David, get alone with your God. Tell Him, "I want to begin life right here, again. Not like Saul, blaming everyone else, pretending, living on a past anointing. But like the son of Jesse . . . willing to be broken . . . cleansed by the blood of Christ . . . living in the light, with my heart set on doing the will of God."

The way to God's heart is the way of brokenness. David walked it; Saul wouldn't. Will you?

Chapter 3

The King's Shepherd

THE "APPLE" IS THE VERY CENTER of the eye. In Old Testament days, when they talked about hurting someone, they spoke of injuring "the apple of his eye." That was bad. Back then there were no bifocals, contact lenses, or ophthalmologists. If you hurt your eye, it was finished—and so were you. That's why people jealously protected their eyes.

The name *David* means "loved one," or "beloved," which is like saying that a person is "the apple of your eye" (Psalm 17:8). David was beloved of God because he was "a man after my own heart" (Acts 13:22). And because of this, his life was marked by greatness. Ever wonder why God included David's biography in the Bible? It wasn't because it was just an interesting story.

Nor was God saying, "Okay, here's the story of my special person. I want you to read it and feel guilty because you'll never measure up—you'll never make it."

A Man After God's Heart

Just the opposite. Someone has well said, "Most books are written for our information, the Bible was written for our transformation." Romans 15:4 puts it this way:

> *For everything that was written in the past was written to teach us, so that through endurance and the encouragement of the Scriptures we might have hope.*

The story of David was recorded to give us encouragement and hope! God loves to walk with men. He longs to speak to the responsive heart. The way to God's heart is wide open through Jesus Christ.

The chronicle of David is simply an account of how one sinful, stumbling human being responded to the grace and love of his Creator. It can be your story, too. I pray that it will be mine.

But what so endeared this man David to his God? What qualities of David's life made him live up to his name being the apple of God's eye?

A THIRST FOR GOD

In 1 Samuel 13, God told the grieving prophet that He would seek out a man after His own heart to take Saul's place on the throne. God continually looks for people who say, "Oh, Lord, I want my heart to be a heart after Your own."

It has nothing to do with whether you're a woman or man, tall or short, young or old. God is looking at you and saying, "Can I use this person? Can I really use this person for My glory? Can I really work through him? Can I give him more opportunities to express the Gospel, win people to

My Son, and build up My Body? Is this person's heart after My own heart? If it is, then I'll keep opening doors for him. I'll use him more and more every day."

God spread an impressive array of opportunities before this young man, David. He was probably eighteen years old when he was anointed to be the founder of the royal line from which Jesus Christ came. Think of it! Out in the pastures among the grazing sheep, God was preparing this teenager to be the founder of Messiah's line. What an indescribable privilege.

A lot of adults look at teenagers today and say, "Oh, those crazy kids." Maybe they are crazy, but there is a lot of beautiful stuff inside those young people—beautiful potential. Certainly there is an ugly side, too—as there is in all of us—and that has to be taken care of by the Lord. But I think David must have gotten the same rub-off when he was a teenager. He was the youngest of eight brothers, and, like normal older brothers, they put him down. When the prophet Samuel came to their ranch house in Bethlehem, they didn't even invite David to the party.

"David? The runt? He's just a kid. He's out with the sheep. Don't bother about him."

But from God's perspective, young David was one of the most important persons in His vast plan of the ages. God looked at David's heart. To his brothers, David was just an irresponsible kid, a wild teenager who beat up lions and scared bears. But God was looking beneath the exterior— and saw a spirit that hungered after Him.

Later on, David became *the* national hero. He came back from leveling Goliath and all the people scrambled to get on the David bandwagon. If it happened today, David T-shirts, wrist bands, baseball caps, bumper stickers, biographies, and CDs would be selling faster than stores could keep them in stock. All the women and girls of Israel sang his praises.

But did this mean much to God? Remember 1 Samuel 16:7?

> *"The LORD does not look at the things man looks at. Man looks on the outward appearance, but the LORD looks at the heart."*

If God sees a heart yearning for His presence, He will withhold no blessing. David was desperate for God. You see it in his life. You hear it in his music.

> *As the deer pants for streams of water,*
> *So my soul pants for you, O God.*
> *My soul thirsts for God, for the living God.*
> *When can I go and meet with God?*
> (Psalm 42:1–2).

> *Oh God, you are my God;*
> *earnestly I seek you:*
> *my soul thirsts for you,*
> *my body longs for you,*
> *in a dry and weary land*
> *where there is no water*
> (Psalm 63:1).

David had the incurable habit of bringing every situation in life to his God. Whether it was a battle, a family decision, a nameless fear, a crushing sorrow, or a cherished dream—whatever it was, the first thing David said was, "I'm going to talk to the Lord about it."

Not that David was some grim-faced grit-your-teeth, pious disciplinarian: "Ah, there's the alarm clock. Have to do my devotions. Have to drag myself out of bed and go through the ritual." None of that at all! With David, it was a natural thing. As soon as the opportunity came up, he spoke with the Lord. In other words, he related everything in his life to the Person of God. He didn't *do* his devotions; he *lived* them.

Take a minute to think through your day, as far as it has progressed. Think about your activities, your words, your purchases, your decisions. How often did you consult your God? How many times today have you paused in your frantic pace to seek the counsel of the One you call "Lord"?

Whether you're a businessman, career woman, house-wife, college student, or high-schooler, you've got to get used to the concept. If we want God to use us in a powerful way, we must have a heart for Him—for His desires, His commands. Everything we do, no matter how trivial or mundane it seems, must relate to His presence and His Person. Then we will realize His blessing.

When it comes to a marriage partner, count on God's provision. Set your heart on God's selection and God's tim-ing. Allow Him to bring along the right man or woman at the right time. Don't take it casually, having decided on some-body and saying, "God, bless so-and-so. I love him. He's got the right kind of eyes. He's ruddy and all the rest of it," and then pray, pray, pray. At that point, it's a tacked-on prayer.

You made your decision before coming to God, instead of the other way around. You're playing games with God. And you may find trouble later on. Deep trouble.

When it comes to money, take the matter to God. Moving from one city to another, take it to God. Changing jobs, really put it before God. Planning a vacation, consult the Lord. You may think, "I'll turn into a fanatic if I start putting God into everything. Only the lunatic fringe does that."

Neglecting to include God in your plans is precisely the reason why so much trouble, agony, and suffering prevail on this planet—because people think they don't have to relate their everyday lives to God. David would bitterly agree.

The few times David neglected to seek God on a matter the results nearly devastated his life and his family. As we'll see later, the chain reaction of pain and sorrow sparked by those few selfish moments gave David pangs for the rest of his life.

A PENETRATING DISCERNMENT

To find out what happened in David's life, we can read the books of Samuel. If we want to know what went on in his mind, we can turn to his own very personal songbook—the Psalms.

Psalm 37 reveals David's unusual inner quality of discernment. In that psalm, David says, "Don't fret because of evil people. Don't worry about the outward appearance. Don't worry about those who prosper and appear to be right even though they are pagans. Don't worry. Their end is coming. They may appear to be well off, but God hasn't settled His accounts yet."

David made that crucial distinction between outward appearance and the heart. Christians are often tempted to think, "Well, look at that man over there. Here I walk with God. I give my tithe to God. I train my children right. And I can hardly cut it at the end of the month. Yet my neighbor over there is a crook. He drinks and runs around. Look at him. He's got money for everything. He can do anything he wants. What's going on?"

In many psalms, David says, "Listen, take time to go into the sanctuary and acknowledge the presence of God. Soon you'll find that outward appearance is not primary. What counts is the reality of being related to God."

It's good to know that when you're a teenager. You know—you go to school and bump into Mr. Muscle or Miss Popularity, the hotshots who push themselves around. They're the girls with a new outfit every week. Or the guys with all the muscles who wear short sleeves to show them off. Maybe you're skinny and wear long sleeves, or else you're short and stubby. But they can do anything they want. If they go to the beach they get a suntan. You go and come back burned and blotchy or peeling like a banana. If they swim, they win the races. If they water ski, they can do it on one—you can't do it with three. Everything seems to go right for them while everything goes upside-down for you.

But the outward appearance doesn't mean much to God. He's looking at your heart. If in your youth God sees a heart that is after His own heart, it will be you who sees the blessing when the full story is told.

A Man After God's Heart

A SENSITIVE SPIRIT

It's not unusual for a man to possess power. Nor is it unusual for power to possess a man. Men and kings are not judged so much for the authority they wield, but rather for how that authority wields them.

In the course of history, many men have found themselves in positions of leadership and command. Some are born to it. Others are elected to it. Still others seize it. Most simply claw their way to the top through long, weary years of sacrifice and toil. All of that is soon forgotten. What is remembered is how that man exercised the power once he obtained it.

God chose Saul to reign. Saul chose to reign without God. In Saul's hand, the authority of the king became hard, brittle, arbitrary, and cruel. Saul held the scepter but the scepter held him. He issued commands simply to command. Clinging to the power of his office, he forfeited the greatest power of all—the presence of God's Spirit. Knowing in his heart that his sovereignty was hollow, the frustrated king rattled his saber all the louder and sought to kill the man who possessed what he had foolishly let slip away.

David, hunted and hounded through years of his early manhood, also found himself in a position of power. In 1 Samuel 24, the Lord placed the life of his mortal enemy, Saul, within his grasp.

> *After Saul returned from pursuing the Philistines, he was told, "David is in the desert of En Gedi." So Saul took three thousand chosen*

men from all Israel and set out to look for David and his men near the Crags of the Wild Goats.

He came to the sheep pens along the way; a cave was there, and Saul went in to relieve himself. David and his men were far back in the cave. (1 Samuel 24:1–3).

Perfect opportunity. What a choice moment for David to rise up and put an end to the man who had sworn to kill him. Saul was unarmed, unsuspecting, and helpless. David's men were going out of their heads for joy. Here was the moment they'd been waiting for. They could hardly keep from shouting. David's man took him aside and whispered tensely:

This is the day the LORD spoke of when he said to you, "I will give your enemy into your hands for you to deal with as you wish" (1 Samuel 24:4).

Why did David delay? "Go get him," they said through clenched teeth. "Butcher him. Cut him down. He's in your hand!" The young shepherd crawled forward in the darkness and cut off a piece of Saul's robe with his razor-sharp dagger. He could just as easily have slipped it between Saul's ribs. David's men must have been stunned with their leader's reaction as he crept back into the depths of the cavern.

Afterward, David was conscience-stricken for having cut off a corner of his robe (1 Samuel 24:5).

Just cutting a piece of the king's robe overwhelmed David's tender conscience. He had touched his knife to the king of Israel—he had reached out his hand against the

51

A Man After God's Heart

Lord's anointed one. It was too much. David forced his men to lie still and let Saul make his exit from the cave. The power had been in David's hand to take vengeance. But David chose to surrender that power to God.

He said, in effect, "If anyone is going to kill Saul it will have to be the Lord, not me. I will not use this moment of power to satisfy my own vengeance. I will not touch the Lord's anointed king." And he let him go. The Lord had given David the power, but instead of being controlled by that power David chose to be controlled by the Lord.

Centuries later, a Son of David would make a similar choice. Surrendering the power that was ever His to exercise, this Descendant of King David allowed Himself to be arrested by wicked men, paraded through a mockery of a trial, and impaled naked and alone on a cruel instrument of death.

> *Who, being in very nature God,*
>   *[he] did not consider equality with God*
>   *something to be grasped,*
> *but made himself nothing,*
>   *taking the very nature of a servant,*
>   *being made in human likeness.*
> *And being found in appearance as a man,*
>   *he humbled himself*
>   *and became obedient to death—*
>   *even death on a cross!*

(Philippians 2:6–8).

> *"Father, if you are willing, take this cup from me; yet not my will, but yours be done"* (Luke 22:42).

A person after God's own heart is one who refuses to take advantage even when it appears that the Lord has set up a situation for him to do precisely that. Perhaps the Lord has placed us in a position of authority where we could suddenly take action against another person who has harmed us. Maybe we're in business and promoted over someone else and we think, "Aha! The moment of opportunity has arrived. Thank the Lord—here's my chance." The temptation seems irresistible.

Once while in Nicaragua, I met a young magazine editor who had received Christ at a Bible study six months before. After a press conference, we had a cup of coffee together and the young journalist revealed a serious struggle he was going through.

"For years," he explained, "two newspaper men have been telling lies about me, trying to destroy me. Just recently I was going through some files and came across some things that could really sink both of these men. In the old days, I wouldn't have hesitated to run a cover-story 'exposé' on these guys."

"And now?" I asked.

"Well . . . now I'm in an awful struggle. Everything in me wants to lash back at those liars—to stick them. But you know, I felt by the Holy Spirit that I shouldn't do it. And yet that goes against all my training. What do you think I should do? Denounce them? Expose them? Really do them in? Or do nothing? I could lose my job if it came out that I sat on this story."

I said, "Now listen. You've obeyed the voice of the Spirit up to now. You'd better do what the Lord tells you to do."

A Man After God's Heart

Although what this editor was going to do was right-eous, the reason he was going to do it was unrighteous. He had enough sensitivity to the Holy Spirit to hold back when he might have easily rammed in the dagger to the hilt. "Just wait on the Lord," I told him. "God has been working these things out down through history. He takes care of it in a beautiful way."

Before the third week of the crusade was over, the editor came back.

"Remember that counsel you gave me about not taking revenge on those two fellows?" he said. "You told me the Lord probably had something planned that was much better—better than I could imagine. Señor Palau, do you know what happened? This week I got a call from the president. I'm being sent out of the country as an assistant ambassador!"

It was so exciting! God had taken care of the situation and the young man was kept from doing something he might have later regretted. His conscience was clear before God. The Bible says in Romans 12:19:

Do not take revenge, my friends, but leave room for God's wrath, for it is written: "It is mine to avenge; I will repay," says the Lord.

It says *never* take your own revenge. You say, "Do you mean *never*? Not even a little bit to show them that I'm not dumb—that I know what's going on?" That's right. It says *never*. God will take care of it.

Now David knew Saul was finished. He knew he was going to be the next king. Even Saul's son Jonathan told him, "You're going to be the king. I'm going to be second

The King's Shepherd

to you." David knew it all—all the prophecies, all the indications. He knew he was going to be Number One. And it appeared normal to human nature to say, "Get him now, and you'll be king today! Why wait any more?"

David had a right to kill Saul. It was war. Saul was out to get him. But David said, "Oh no. I'm not going to move one step ahead of the Lord." He was sensitive. The same position of power that had turned Saul's heart from God turned David's heart to greater reliance upon his Lord. David's influence and might would greatly eclipse that of his predecessor, but it was a tempered strength—tempered by gentleness and by sensitivity to God's Spirit.

Think about it for a minute. What is your reaction when God places you in a position of power? You say, "What power? I'm no king. I don't carry a sword around." No, but we all find ourselves in a position of advantage from time to time; as an officeholder at church, as a supervisor at work, as a parent, or as a wife or husband who knows right where that partner is most vulnerable. The moment of advantage— how we respond in that instant of power—reveals volumes about our character and our walk with God.

David surrendered his opportunity, his power, and his advantage to God. He turned back from following after vengeance, and kept right on pursuing God's heart. Which way are you running?

A WILLINGNESS TO ADMIT SIN

If Saul had not been king, he could have blamed all his troubles on the government. Unfortunately, he *was* the government. So he blamed the people instead. Constantly.

Saul would tell God, "It's because of these people that such-and-such happened. I was just trying to please the people." He even had the audacity to blame Samuel the prophet. Saul said, "Well, you didn't show up on time. What else could I do?" Saul never admitted his sins; he was always quick to justify himself.

Not so with David. When the prophet pointed the finger at David's sin, it was like a hot poker on his chest. He cried out to God. In his spirit, he could immediately discern when God was speaking to him through another person.

In 1 Samuel 25, the one who spoke was a woman named Abigail. This brave woman stepped out in front of a vengeance-bent 400-man army, with David leading the pack. Putting yourself in the path of an inflamed company of fierce swordsmen would be like leaping from a subway platform in front of a speeding train. In those days, men of war didn't have much time for pleading women, especially when they were in the way. But Abigail was no ordinary woman and David was no average soldier. Plus, Abigail had a message.

Her foolish husband, Nabal, had just delivered a stinging rebuke to the exiled son of Jesse, returning David's kindness with a cold, insulting refusal to help. David's response?

"Put on your swords!" So they put on their swords, and David put on his. About four hundred men went up with David (1 Samuel 25:13).

David was on fire and his eyes were filled with visions of liquidating a wooden-headed sheep-rancher named Nabal.

Abigail, Nabal's unfortunate wife, got wind of the plan and immediately mounted her donkey in hopes of intercepting David's hardened bank of outcast soldiers. Seeing David striding forward in a fury, Abigail jumped off her donkey and bowed at David's feet. She knew David could have hewed her in two with his sword or trampled over the top of her. When he didn't, she took that as a good sign and spoke up. In essence, she said:

"Sir, I know my husband is a mule and all that. I realize he deserves to be killed. But when you become king, what will happen to your memory if you cut down this foolish man? What will people say about you? You will have a stain on your hands. I beg you not to touch him. God will judge my husband."

David cooled down fast. The murderous anger faded from his eyes and he regarded this remarkable woman with amazement and appreciation. Recognizing the voice of God in Abigail's plea, David replied:

> *"Praise be to the LORD, the God of Israel, who has sent you today to meet me. May you be blessed for your good judgment and for keeping me this day from bloodshed this day and from avenging myself with my own hands. Otherwise, as surely as the LORD the God of Israel, lives, who has kept me from harming you, if you had not come quickly to meet me, not one male belonging to Nabal would have been left alive by daybreak"* (1 Samuel 25:32–34).

Here was a woman David had never met. And when she pointed out to him the folly of his course, the most feared man in Israel replied, "Thank you for coming. Thank you for stopping me. You are right. It would have been a mistake."

A Man After God's Heart

God took care of the situation; about ten days later her husband Nabal died. Later on, David sent for Abigail and she willingly became his wife.

In Psalm 51 David said, "A broken and contrite heart, O God, you will not despise." David always had a broken heart over his sin. He didn't point the finger like Saul—he allowed the finger to point at him. Even when he was king, on top of the pile, again and again David would come down from his throne, get on his knees, and admit, "I have sinned against the Lord." And the Lord always forgave him. You never find David defending himself like Saul did. You never see him trying to justify his own guilt. As soon as a sin or weakness was pointed out, he'd say, "You're right. I am to blame. God forgive me." That's the big difference.

So many people want to defend themselves, refusing to admit their guilt. We see homosexual activists deny their sin and seek to explain away the clear and ringing words of Scripture. It's the same with adultery. More and more people arrogantly challenge the strong voice of God's Word and say, "What's wrong with divorcing my wife and marrying another woman? God wants me to be happy. God wants me to have peace." Far worse than defending their sin is the arrogance of defying God to His face.

But when a person who has sinned is truly broken before God, agreeing with God over his sin and willing to change his direction, he will find cleansing and healing. The Lord is the first one (and in many cases the only one) to forgive him.

Have you ever had a broken heart over your sins? Have you ever really wept before the Lord? Not necessarily real tears, but inward tears—for your own sinfulness, agreeing with God that you were wrong?

David was not perfect, but he longed to be perfect. He desired to be holy. He prayed:

Search me, O God, and know my heart;
*   test me and know my anxious thoughts.*
See if there is any offensive way in me,
*   and lead me in the way everlasting*
(Psalm 139:23–24).

David not only agreed with God about his sins, in his heart he also wanted to agree with God about holiness. In Psalm 139 he says, in effect, "Oh God, Your thoughts are so beautiful. I could just spend hours counting them. If I start adding them up, they are more than the sand. Oh Lord, I hate sin, I hate it in others. I hate it in myself. Teach me, search my motives and my thoughts. Lord, show me what doesn't belong. Show me what makes You sad as You examine my life."

David was a soldier, a general, an ambitious character—but he was also a man with a tender heart who wanted to be holy.

Do you want to be holy? Or do you say, "Oh, forget holiness. It's too old-fashioned"? Do you long to be holy? Of course, we all have impure thoughts, and they often attack us when we're least expecting them. We all have moments when our attitudes are ugly and we hate ourselves for it. But the big question is this: Do you *want* to be holy? Do you *want* to be pure? Do you long to be clean? Do you long to be transparent before God and before people?

A Man After God's Heart

Get alone with God. Pray, "Oh God, I want to love holiness. Teach me how to be holy. Train my spirit to be thirsty for it like David was thirsty for it." As Christians, we are indwelt by God's Holy Spirit. Can you imagine a better teacher?

A HAPPY AND WORSHIPFUL HEART

We could note many other qualities of David that made him a man after God's heart. For one, David had a happy spirit. This doesn't mean he was *never* sorrowful or angry. David had plenty of opportunities to grieve—more than most of us. But there was something magnetic about him. He was the kind of man who could take 400 bitter outcasts and rebels into his following and before the year was out, transform them into a loyal army.

You can sense it in many of his psalms. Whether he was out in the hills, hiding in a cave, in the midst of battle, or sitting on his throne, David would pour out his heart to God. When he did, there was always room for praise and always room for getting excited about the greatness of God and His grace.

Sometimes it helps if we read these psalms in a translation different from the one we're used to. Otherwise, they become so familiar that they just roll off our tongues and never penetrate our hearts. Reading them in another translation can make David's diary leap off the page at us. I grew up with the Spanish Bible; this translation to me is like the New International Version to many other people. I've known the Spanish Bible since preschool days. I could almost beat David to it when I'm reading. But when I get into a modern English translation, it's so refreshing it seems completely new.

What is it like to live with *you*, to work next to *you* day after day? If you were to suddenly be taken to heaven, how would those who had been near you characterize your life? As a man with a happy and worshipful heart? As a woman who was a joy to be around?

David was excited about life—excited about being a servant of God. And you know what? The Lord loves that. The Lord loves people. He is searching for those who will worship Him in spirit and in truth.

Chapter 4

The Shepherd King

BEFORE CONSIDERING THE SHEPHERD KING, we had to look at the King's shepherd. Before we examined David over men it was necessary to see David under God. Now, having seen the man after God's own heart, we're ready to look at the king of God's own choice.

"YOU DID NOT CHOOSE ME . . ."

Remember what God said to Samuel after Saul had ruined his reign over Israel?

> *"How long will you mourn for Saul, since I have rejected him as king over Israel? Fill your horn with oil, and be on your way; I am sending you to Jesse of Bethlehem. I have chosen one of his sons to be king"* (1 Samuel 16:1).

A Man After God's Heart

How did David become king? The Lord said, *I have selected him.* David didn't become king because he pushed himself into it. He became king because God selected him to become king. It wasn't because some big-name prophet laid hands on David or poured oil over him and said, "This is he!" No, the son of Jesse was God's choice for the job.

When the prophet put his hands on him it was just a confirmation of something the Lord had already settled. It was public affirmation before David's whole family, because otherwise they'd never have believed him. But as far as God was concerned, He had selected David while the teenager was still out in the hills with his father's sheep.

What a beautiful phrase: "I have selected a king for Myself." Don't leave those words in Hebrew history; don't file them away in a folder marked "Interesting Phrases." Remember, He's selected you, too!

In John 15, Jesus, the Son of David, said:

You did not choose me, but I chose you and appointed you to go and bear fruit (verse 16).

As those who belong to Jesus Christ, each of us can point back to a moment of decision in our lives, whether or not we remember the exact date and details. Maybe it was at a crusade or a camp or a church meeting, or maybe just alone in your kitchen. Wherever it was, at that moment, you gave your life to the Lord. That was your moment of decision, but the fact is, you were selected by God. What a comforting thought! I can never get over it.

As I write these words, I am here because God selected me. And He's selected you. Don't wear yourself out trying to understand that concept. Just let it open a refresh-ing spring of encouragement in your spirit—right now.

The Lord says, "I want you to be one of My own. I want you to be a king." Revelation 1:6 tells us that we are "kings and priests unto God." In other words, we can be kingly in our ways. Remember that! As a child of God you have dignity and infinite worth. You're not a worm, not some lowly creature who has to walk about all hunched over looking beaten and humiliated. You were selected by the King of kings and given a task that has implications for all eternity, no matter who you are, no matter how unimportant and insignificant you seem by your own estimation.

The Lord not only selected David to be king, but in 1 Samuel 16:3 He says:

> *Invite Jesse to the sacrifice, and I will show you what you to do. You are to anoint for me the one I indicate.*

God not only selected David, He anointed him. Bible teachers frequently point out that the anointing of oil is a picture of the Holy Spirit's presence in the lives of Christians. Each one of us who belongs to Christ has been selected and anointed by God Himself.

This anointing, this fullness of the Holy Spirit, is not something to flaunt before others. Rather, it is some-thing to offer up to the Lord with gratitude and praise. We should say, "Lord Jesus, when You anointed me with Your Spirit, You anointed me for Your honor, for Yourself. Glory to Your name!"

A Man After God's Heart

Remember these things when your Enemy, Satan, whispers in your ear that you are worthless and nothing in God's sight. It's a lie!

A Love for Uniting the Nation

As the king of God's choice, David was gripped by the desire to bring unity to his fragmented country.

Even today, Israel is one of the most divided nations on the face of the earth. Back then, each of the twelve tribes was always fighting the other. Even though the tribes were supposed to be one nation under God (to borrow a familiar phrase), they weren't. Judges would come and go. Judah would fight against this one and Reuben would fight against another. Only when an outside enemy attacked them would they unite to help one another.

Doesn't that sound like the denominational scene we see in churches today? You know, we resign ourselves to division until an outside enemy crashes in and threatens the whole church. Then it's, "Come on, let's huddle! Let's work together before we get our heads blown off."

As I've traveled around the world, I've been interested to see that in countries where the church is persecuted, people immediately forget about labels. They never ask, "Are you Presbyterian, Nazarene, Methodist, Mennonite, Lutheran, Foursquare, Brethren, Baptist, Assemblies of God, Anglican, or something else?" No, they're just a little band of believers who help each other, hide each other, and cling together like brothers and sisters. And they are.

When David came to power in Israel, one of his great desires was to destroy the internal enemies and unite the nation. Remember, when the people of Israel came out of Egypt, God said, "Look, this is the territory I'm going to give to you. You move in step by step and take the land. You must completely push out all the people who are in the land that belongs to you."

But the people of Israel didn't do that. They (like Saul) kept the best of this and the best of that. They forgave this bunch and they forgave that bunch. Later on, all these forgiven bunches they'd been told to exterminate became their worst enemies. When David took over the throne, he was firmly committed to carry out the order God issued to the Israelites hundreds of years before, to wipe the land clean of internal enemies. He wanted to rid Israel of idolatry and make the nation one.

And he did. By the grace of God, by the power of Jehovah, he took to war. He began to destroy the Philistines, the Amalekites, and all the rest you read about. When his son Solomon came to the throne, the land was at peace and united. As Solomon ascended to power, his era would become a type—a picture—of the millennial reign of Christ. The son of David ruled over a peaceful, united kingdom.

David, a man after God's own heart, a king of God's own choice, had a deep inner desire for unity. He wanted Israel to become all God intended it to be and he knew that could happen only when the nation was one. This is an important parallel for Christians.

You can never be fully a person after God's own heart if you can't tolerate members of the Body of Christ. If they are born again, if they are redeemed by the death of Jesus on the cross, they are part of the Body of Christ just like you.

A Man After God's Heart

LOVE THE WHOLE BODY

Many people love like the Pharisees. They love those who love them. But they have no tolerance at all for anybody who is "different." Few people love *all* the Body of Christ. Those who do, rise quickly to the top into positions of church leadership. I've seen it happen again and again as I've traveled in scores of countries around the world.

Very, very few people truly accept and love a brother in Christ simply because he is a brother in Christ. Usually they get to talking and start cutting up the pie over certain beliefs and practices—Calvinism or Arminianism, Pentecostal or non-Pentecostal, Dispensational or Reformed, Traditional or Contemporary—and on it goes.

Acts 20:28 says very clearly that the church—the Body of our Lord Jesus Christ—was purchased with Christ's own blood. Listen, if Jesus Christ bought me with His priceless blood and if someone doesn't like me, he is going to have a hard time facing Jesus Christ. Because Jesus gave His blood for me, that means I cost Him something. And He is going to love me even if I do make mistakes . . . and I do. He also redeemed you, even if you're obnoxious and hard to get along with. If you are redeemed, I will love you because you are redeemed.

Do you long to be God's person? If so, you ought to love the whole Body of Christ. This doesn't mean you'll agree on everything. Nor does it mean you'll go around approving everything everybody else is doing. It isn't some phony "love-for-all-mankind" sort of sentiment. It's not necessarily an emotional thing at all. It is rather allowing the Spirit of Christ to so control you that His love for His

Body flows through you. Are you willing to allow Him to do this in your life?

I know many people who are just one step from breaking through to being great leaders, great servants of God, with great influence. Some of them are close friends of mine. But they will not budge on this one thing. They prefer to be anti-this or anti-that. And God will not—and cannot—pour out His full blessing on someone who doesn't genuinely love everyone redeemed by the blood of the cross.

Think about this truth—let it grip you—before you settle back into the comfort and security of your little denominational corner. The issues at stake are greater than you imagine.

GOD AT THE CENTER

How often a simple, youthful walk with God becomes clouded and obscured by advancing age and success. If anyone could be rated a prime candidate for this sort of decline it would have to be David.

After all, it is one thing to walk with God when you're a lonely teenage boy out in the wilderness with a flock of sheep. You would expect a certain amount of religious fervor from a sensitive young man who listened with awe to the rumbling thunderstorms and stayed awake in the night watching the stars.

But what happens when the youthful exuberance begins to wear off? What happens when the young man is thrust into the public spotlight and weighed down with the responsibilities of family and government? What happens when the poor boy becomes a wealthy man and the lonely teenager becomes a national hero? What happens to zeal for God then?

Nothing, as far as David was concerned. The boy after God's own heart grew into the man after God's own heart. The zealous teenager became the zealous king. When David was a shepherd in the hill country he made it his practice to put Jehovah at the center of his thoughts, his songs, his joy, and his dreams. God was the center of his personal life. As king of all Israel, it was natural for the son of Jesse to make sure God was at the very center of national life as well. One way he did this was by bringing the Ark of the Covenant to the national capital.

You will remember the Ark of the Covenant was constructed for tabernacle worship while the children of Israel were still wandering with Moses in the wilderness. In their worship, it was a picture of God's presence. Indeed, God actually promised to speak to the children of Israel from the mercy seat between the wings of the cherubim adorning the top of the Ark. The Ark was placed in a separate room of the tabernacle called the Holy of Holies, which only the high priest could enter once a year. In this way, God met His people.

Carried into Canaan, the Ark was soon disregarded by the people of Israel. Later, during the time of the judges, they practically forgot the presence of God. The Ark was off somewhere. Nobody paid much attention to it except from time to time when some judge would come to shake things up a bit. Most of the time, however, the Ark was forgotten and the Lord was not in the center of national life.

When David became king, the nation of Israel was so bruised and battered by wars, troubles, and divisions that

God's presence was only a distant memory. With God out of the center, Israel lost its stability, unity, and national purpose. Drifting back and forth on the tides of human power and opinion, Israel's ship of state weathered constant bickering, animosity, and open hostility among the people.

And doesn't that happen among us, when a congregation of believers forgets it true focus? A church has some trouble and people gossip, talk, and debate. They call special meetings and stay up until midnight. But actually their minds are already set in their own opinions—they are remembering the Lord very little.

Some relatives of mine had this sort of thing going on in their church. As I listened to them talk I thought to myself, "Thank you, Lord, for getting me out of that kind of circle." Their church was fighting over concerns of little consequence. They were obsessed with rule-keeping, ready to dismiss a young pastor over some petty issue. He hadn't done anything wrong. Yet there wasn't any talk about the resurrection of the Lord Jesus, or of the great acts of God in our time, or about the power of the Holy Spirit, or of people coming to Christ.

Like a band of self-proclaimed vigilantes, these people went riding around the neighborhood on their white horses looking for specks in the eyes of their brethren. How foolish! Consumed with all the "negatives," their eyes wandered from the great Positive in their very midst. Like the Israelites in the day of the judges, they lost their true focus and the great overriding purpose for their existence. And where was the Lord? Well, He certainly wasn't in the center.

A Man After God's Heart

I remember one church business meeting I attended. It was really sad. One man got up and said, "The pastor has to go because of this and that." Then a woman got up and said, "That's right. Amen, brother." Weeping, the pastor's daughter got up and said, "My father is a good man. Why do you treat him this way?" On and on it went, into the night. Fighting, angry, bitter words. I thought, "Lord, is this the church of the living God? Listen to them!"

So often we forget divisions arise because God doesn't have His rightful place in our midst. When the worship of God becomes secondary, bickering becomes primary. It happens every time. David saw this in Israel.

The young king's excitement was boundless as he brought the neglected and forgotten Ark back into a place of prominence in the City of David.

> *David and the whole house of Israel were celebrating with all their might before the Lord, with songs and with harps, lyres, tambourines, sistrums, and cymbals . . . . David . . . danced before the LORD with all his might, while he and the entire house of Israel brought up the ark of the LORD with shouts and the sound of trumpets* (2 Samuel 6:5, 14–15).

What a celebration! No one fell asleep in that service! Not a single husband thought about the football game he was missing on television. Not a single wife worried about the roast in the oven. And David? He forgot all about royal dignity and protocol. He didn't worry in the least about his public image. The ark of the living

God was coming into town! And David danced "with all his might."

With every ounce of strength and emotional intensity he possessed, David welcomed the return of God to His rightful place in Israel . . . at the center. Bringing back the ark was to be the first step of David's lifelong cherished dream: to build a temple for his God.

God is looking for people who dream those sorts of dreams, people who long for his glory. He wants to use people like David who put the Lord at the absolute center of their lives and goals. That's why God said of David, "Now there is a man after My own heart. He stumbles, he fails Me from time to time, but I can see the desire of his soul. He wants to put Me first—he wants to make Me the center."

Could you honestly say that about your life—your heart? It's one thing to stand up in a testimony meeting and say, "Ah yes, Jesus is Lord . . . . Amen." But deep down—in your inner self—is it true that Jesus Christ is the center? Is He in the center of your plans? The center of your family? The center of your hopes and dreams? Does He fill your vision? Do you honestly have that inner confidence and rest that, no matter what you are going through, the Lord Jesus is dwelling in your heart by faith?

Listen to how Paul expressed it:

> *I have been crucified with Christ: and I no longer live, but Christ lives in me. The life I live in the body, I live by faith in the Son of God, who loved me and gave himself for me* (Galatians 2:20).

A Man After God's Heart

David had that confidence that the Lord was at the center of his life. And the Lord poured out the blessing. Do you want the blessing of God on your life, your family? Take time for a spiritual inventory. What is it that dominates your dreams and fills your vision? Do you find your inner self cluttered with selfish ambitions and materialistic goals? Bring God back where He belongs. Place Him at the center. He has a way of putting a cluttered house in order.

SEEKING GOD'S MIND

A third quality of David's reign as king of Israel and king of God's choice is that he actively and persistently sought God's mind on military decisions. In 1 Samuel 23, David rescued the town of Keilah from an invading force of Philistines only to find himself the object of an intense manhunt mounted by King Saul and David's fellow Israelites. On both occasions David sought the mind of God.

In other words, he didn't say, "All right, boys, here's another crusade. Let's hit it. It's the will of God that we destroy these heretics. So let's go get them." No. He said, "Let's see what the Lord has to say."

> *[David] inquired of the Lord, saying, "Shall I go and attack these Philistines?" The Lord answered him, "Go, attack and Philistines and save Keilah"* (1 Samuel 23:2).

But David's men were restless when he broke the news to them. They weren't so sure they wanted to risk a commando raid on Keilah.

"We're running like rabbits from Israel's army and you talk about attacking Philistines?"

That shook David up a little, so he went back to the Lord for confirmation. He said, "Lord, my friends say we shouldn't go. What do you say again? Okay, we'll go." It's beautiful to listen in on their conversation.

Even though David had fought many battles, defeating Goliath, the Philistines, and many other enemies, he didn't depend on old victories for new battles. David went back to the Lord for fresh instructions.

In my work as an evangelist, I must remind myself of how David constantly prayed over the battle he was facing. Often in our international crusades we find ourselves facing major decisions. In our excitement over a possible course of action, we're tempted sometimes to say, "Oh, we don't have to ask the Lord about this one. It's so obvious." Then when we fall flat on our faces and wonder what happened, it's obvious. Instead of consulting the Lord we went ahead with the "obvious," which wasn't necessarily God's best for the moment.

If David had only applied this same principle to his domestic life—how different his family history might have been. David committed his military decisions to the Lord, but he neglected to consult God regarding marriage. He simply didn't pray about the women in his life. And that severely crippled his effectiveness for God.

This has happened to many people . . . not just David. People will pray about a job, a church, unsaved relatives, and the Sunday school lesson. But when it comes to choosing a girlfriend (or a boyfriend), they think, "That's my choice. God doesn't have to be involved." So they refuse, or carefully neglect, to speak to the Lord about this portion of their lives.

In Proverbs we read:

Above all else, guard your heart,
for it is the wellspring of life
(Proverbs 4:23).

Often Christian parents neglect to commit this area of their children's lives to earnest prayer. They have their own ideas of what they want for their son or daughter. If it's a daughter, they'll want her to marry a sharp doctor with a Porsche and a new boat in the garage. Praying about it gets a little touchy. They say instead, "Let's just trust the Lord . . . but go ahead and do it." So young people rush into marriage but in ten months or perhaps ten years they come back for counseling. Maybe they didn't marry that doctor but rather someone else they didn't pray about—and he or she turned out to be a drunk, an adulterer, or something else.

We need to learn from David's life—his triumphs— *and* his mistakes. That's why the Bible records all of it for us, so that we can profit from this man's heart for God and avoid the tragedies that nearly ruined him.

A SERVANT'S HEART

From man's perspective, the tools one needs to carve out a position of leadership in the world include a good-looking face, lots of charisma, regular press bulletins, and a media-wise public relations man.

But don't try to use those tools to get ahead in the kingdom of God. It won't work. The Holy Spirit won't allow it.

What God looks for in the leader of His choice is a servant's heart. And if you have a servant's heart you can be greatly used of the Lord.

The servant heart of David was in evidence from his early teenage years. While young David served his father in the fields with the sheep, the other sons of Jesse were trying army careers. Eliab, Abinadab, Shammah, and the rest of them would come home on a three-day liberty, strutting around town in their flashy uniforms, but David—well, you know— he was out with the sheep. Nevertheless, while Jesse's older sons were out on training maneuvers with King Saul, David was alone in the hills being trained by the God of Israel.

Isn't it great the way God ignores all the man-made rules to fulfill His perfect will? That's the exciting thing about following Christ. He's never worried about doing things in the expected way, going through all the ordinary channels. God finds His own channels. God writes His own methods.

Sometimes we'd like to present God with our operating manual and tell Him, "Now, this is the way it's done. These are the rules. This is the kind of person for the job." But God chooses His own leaders! He doesn't care one whit if a man is a shepherd, or a fig picker, or a fisherman, or a tax collector. God is looking for a responsive heart. Ask Rahab the harlot. God isn't impressed in the least by job title, bank account, or standing in the community.

God is searching for a servant's heart. And looking out across the hills of Israel, God's gaze went right past the eldest son, Eliab, with his flashy uniform, to let His eyes rest on a teenage shepherd. "Here's a man after my own heart," God said. "This lad is going to be king of all of them."

A Man After God's Heart

David could have said, "But Lord, taking care of sheep? Following them through the wilderness? How can I ever become king?" But it was right there in the pasture that the Lord was teaching him to be king. His hotshot brothers who were pushing their own careers, trying to step all over David, never got to be anything. When David came out to the battlefront they said, "What are you doing, showing off here? Get out of here, kid. Go back to your sheep." But after the Goliath incident, do you hear about the brothers any more? It's hard to even remember their names, isn't it?

When David's father asked him to carry some food to his brothers on the battlefield, he could have said, "Why should I take food to those guys? They're always putting me down. I don't like them. Send one of the slaves." But David didn't say that. He said. "Yes, Father, I'll go." By obeying and carrying that picnic lunch to his brothers, what happened? He met Goliath.

If David hadn't obeyed and done what Jesse asked him to do, he'd never have been on the battlefield at the right time, in the perfect timing of God. He would never have defeated Goliath and, humanly speaking, he would have spent the rest of his life taking care of sheep. But because he followed through, step by step, and he had a servant's heart in his tender years, everything fell into place. God saw to it.

You'll notice, too, that when David was asked to become an assistant to King Saul he had a humble servant's heart. David already knew he would be the next king. He'd already been anointed with oil by Samuel. And when they asked him to play the lyre, to soothe Saul's jangled nerves, he did it without a murmur.

David didn't say, "Hey, listen, I'm the one who silenced that loud-mouthed Goliath. All the girls are singing songs about me. Why should I sit here playing the lyre for this nervous old king?"

Instead he said, "All right, if I've got to play for this king who's trying to kill me, I'll play."

FAITHFUL IN LITTLE THINGS

The Bible says the person who is faithful in little things will also be faithful in much. Think about that. It was a "little thing" for David to faithfully tend his father's sheep, wasn't it? Yet, God was watching him. It was a "little thing" to carry a few loaves of bread to the battle line for his brothers. But God was preparing a marvelous opportunity for him.

What is a "little thing" and what is a "big thing"? Are there really little things, little responsibilities, little jobs in the service of Jesus Christ? Remember, our God doesn't measure as we measure. We look at publicity, national acclaim, and the public spotlight as the measure of success. God looks at faithfulness. What little things has God asked you to do? What little responsibilities have you been charged with? Do you feel neglected . . . shelved . . . forgotten? Give your task to God. Ask Him to help you attack it in His strength, with His perspective, reflecting His joy.

There are many great names in this world, attracting great attention and drawing great acclaim. God looks right past them in His search for little people in little jobs with great faithfulness and a great heart for Him. Are His eyes resting on you?

A Man After God's Heart

A SHEPHERD'S HEART

Finally, we could note a fifth quality in David's reign as king of God's choice. The son of Jesse had a tender shepherd's heart for his people. He may have been a rugged soldier who climbed all over the mountains of Judah like a wild goat. He may have been a politician who knew how to work the system and who could be cold and hard at times as the situation demanded. But in his heart, David loved the people of Israel. There was a tenderness there that you may find surprising. He even called the people . . . sheep.

This started back when he was a teenager and went against a gorilla-like warrior named Goliath. He went out and said, "This Philistine is taunting the armies of God. He's a reproach to all of Israel. I'm going to tackle him in the name of the Lord."

He loved the people of Israel even when they were rotten, unruly, and ungrateful. Many of those people he risked his life fighting for didn't even want him as their king. In fact, for seven-and-a-half years after Saul died, only the tribe of Judah and Benjamin acknowledged him as king. Some of them said, "Who is David? Who is the son of Jesse?" Yet he continued to love the nation. When the rest of the tribes finally came around and acknowledged him as ruler, he didn't say, "Hey, where were you guys seven years ago? Now go fly a kite." Not David. Very humbly he said, "All right. I'll be king over you, too, if you want."

The depth of this man's love for the people is seen in his reign. For example, 1 Chronicles 21 relates the incident where Satan tempted David to take pride in the number of people in his kingdom. There is nothing inherently wrong with taking a census or keeping statistics. In fact, on another occasion God *commanded* David to count the people, even as He had commanded Moses to number the people at another point in Israel's history. What mattered here, however, was the *reason* David wanted to count the people. It was a matter of sinful pride.

It seems it wasn't only David who got cocky about the big numbers, but also the people of Israel. They thought, "Look at that population figure. We are a big nation now. We can really defend our frontiers from the enemy. We can hold up our heads on the world scene. We've got the strength. We've got all these soldiers to fight the enemies. We've got David as general, Abner as his assistant. We can do it alone."

But God wasn't pleased. Even as the last figures from the last village were being tallied, God's anger fell upon David and the whole nation. He sent a pestilence, killing 70,000 people. They were dropping right and left.

> *David looked up and saw the angel of the LORD standing between heaven and earth, with a drawn sword in his hand extended over Jerusalem. Then David and the elders, clothed in sackcloth, fell facedown.*
>
> *David said to God, "Was it not I who ordered the fighting men to be counted? I am the one who has sinned and done wrong. These are but sheep. What have they done? O LORD my God, let your hand fall upon me and my family, but do not let this plague remain upon your people"*
> (1 Chronicles 21:16–17).

A Man After God's Heart

This is a touching incident. Remember, David wasn't afraid of blood. He'd killed plenty of people in battle and in raids on towns of enemies. But here he was faced with the knowledge that he had sinned against God. As a result, God was bringing a pestilence on the whole nation. David prayed, "Oh Lord, it's me. Chastise me. Punish me. Leave the sheep alone. I'm the only one who has it coming."

Notice that you don't find David praying, "Well, they had it coming, too. They're sinners. Let the Lord do it His way."

No, David really prayed his heart out for the people. He loved them like a shepherd. And God heard his prayer and stopped the pestilence.

It is interesting to compare David with his son Solomon who was, in human terms, the greatest king in Israel's history. With his matchless wisdom and administrative genius, Solomon had the nation running like a precision timepiece. Besides that, Solomon had wealth and power and worldwide fame that his father never dreamed of. Both men figure highly in the annals of the nation called Israel. But only one was a man after God's own heart. And it wasn't Solomon.

Why not open your Bible and make your own list of character qualities from the life of this man David? Answer the question yourself: What made David a man after God's own heart? But don't stop there. It wasn't just for the sake of history that God left the list for us to discover.

Down through the ages, God has been looking for other men and women to leave mediocrity behind and follow Him with a whole heart.

He's still looking.

Chapter 5

All the King's Horses, All the King's Men

REMEMBER THE FALL OF SAUL? It didn't happen in one cataclysmic tumble—one dam burst deluge. It wasn't as if one morning over his oatmeal Saul decided he would reject God and rebel against His prophets.

Sin didn't destroy Saul in a flash flood—it ate him away by erosion. It wasn't a sudden house fire, it was more like termites. Maintaining his kingly exterior, Saul went empty inside. One sin led to another sin, one lie to another lie, one jealousy to another, one disobedience to another. Finally, there wasn't much left for the Philistines to conquer.

But then, you say, the fall of David must have been different. With Saul it was like a slow rust but with David it must have been like an instant crash. Like a falling star.

83

A Man After God's Heart

After all, wasn't he the man after God's own heart? He must have taken his eyes off the road a minute, then—boom—he was in the ditch.

It didn't happen that way. No one falls "suddenly." Not even David. Remember this: David's great sin did not happen in one impetuous, impulsive, momentous outburst of passion. David, like Saul, fell because of unjudged sin that finally caught up to blur his vision at a crucial moment.

Someone once told me, "Nobody becomes a Marxist overnight. You go slowly from the right to the left, and one morning you wake up and realize you're a committed Marxist."

In the same way, nobody gets fat overnight. It's one pizza after another, one triple scoop ice cream cone after another. And you hardly notice it until one of your children comes up, pokes you in the stomach, and says, "Dad, you've got a big belly."

Immorality begins with tiny things sown in your youth. Little things, little attitudes, little habits. Maybe some casual petting on a date, maybe some pornography that fell into your hands, maybe a fascination for sensual novels and stories. Little things. Yet if you don't crucify them—if you don't bring them to judgment—if you don't face them as the sins that they are, they can destroy you. They can blur your moral judgment at a crucial, irreversible juncture in life.

When the massive Teton Dam in southeastern Idaho collapsed, everyone was stunned. Without warning, under clear skies, the huge earthen structure suddenly gave way, sending millions of gallons of water surging into the Snake

River basin. A sudden catastrophe? An instantaneous disaster? It certainly seemed to be, from all outward appearances.

Yet underneath, below the waterline where the engineers at the Teton Dam couldn't see, a hidden fault had been ever-so-gradually weakening the entire structure. It started small enough. Just a little weak spot, a little bit of erosion. No one saw it and it went untended. By the time the fault was detected, it was too late. The workmen on the dam barely had time to run for their lives and escape being swept away. No one saw the little flaw, but everyone saw the big collapse.

The record of David's moral collapse is recorded in 2 Samuel 11:1–12:15. It's all there, all the sordid details. We open our mouths in stunned silence as we read how "the man after God's own heart" raped another man's wife, tried to cover his dirty tracks, then turned around and murdered the woman's husband. We say, "How could it happen? David? The Sweet Psalmist of Israel? I can't believe it."

We hear the same reaction in churches today when some glaring incident of sexual immorality within the assembly comes to the surface and takes everyone by surprise.

"Ahh—my! Such a fine-looking woman. Dressed nicely, was a good mom, always took notes on the sermons, always listened to Bible cassettes in the car. And *she* ran off with *Harold?* Why, I was there when Harold was baptized. How could he do that? How could they do this?"

Some people say, "Well, they just stumbled." Come on, now. They didn't stumble. It was a planned move. The loud collapse that masks the hidden, neglected crack in the dam.

A Man After God's Heart

In soccer there's a little move some of the players use when the referee is looking the other way. They know how to deftly put a foot out to the side and trip another player who is running full-throttle downfield. It's quick, neat, and hard to spot when a player pulls it off. It looks just like the other guy stumbled over his own feet. When you talk about stumbling, people get the impression this innocent young thing was just walking along when Satan put out a foot and—wham! She just fell over and . . . what can you say? You've heard the lines people come up with:

"Forgive me, dear husband. It wasn't a big thing. I'll never see the guy again."

"Elders of the church, it was just a little fall. You know how it is . . . I didn't mean it. Just receive me at the Lord's Table again and it'll all be okay. I'm through with this other man . . . I just . . . stumbled."

Nonsense. Nobody falls into sex sin by chance. Nobody commits fornication, adultery, or a homosexual act out of one sudden blast hitting him from somewhere. It builds up slowly, slowly, slowly. Falling is just the effect of the cumulative bundle of temptation and passion that has been piling up and has not been crucified. When the person falls, go ahead and weep for him or her, but not in that weak, sentimental sense of wanting to cover things over. That person needs to bring his sin to the cross, to be broken before God, confessing it all. She must recognize that her sin is a loathsome thing in the sight of a holy God.

If we aren't hard on sin, people will never break. They will try to pass it off. I've had people counsel me, "Tread easy, Luis. Tone it down a little. Some of these people have suffered enough—you'll hurt their feelings." Yet allowing sin to be shoved to one side isn't helping the person at all—it's hurting him—dreadfully.

The sin of immorality is a killing, cancerous thing. You're not doing any good for the person at all until you've helped her see that she must be genuinely broken before God. Once the sin has been dealt with by the Lord, then the healing will come. But not until.

I Surrender All (Except . . .)

But how did it happen to David? How is it that God's hand-picked king failed so tragically? It really started years before, when David was young.

Reviewing his remarkable life story, we see that the son of Jesse was a man committed to prayer. David prayed over nearly everything. He prayed before battles and after battles. He prayed about his enemies and his friends. He prayed for direction and dedication, for health and for happiness, in his highs and in his lows, in caves and in castles.

David poured out everything before God. Except—never once in the Bible do you find David praying about his love life. Not once. Although he ended up with eight wives and numerous concubines, we have no record that David took these prospective marriages before God, seeking His counsel. It was one area of his life that he never yielded, and it almost crushed him.

As human beings, we are composed of three parts: body, soul, and spirit. The spirit puts us in touch with God. The soul is our personality, the sum of intellect, emotions, and will.

A Man After God's Heart

David had a beautiful *spirit*. As you read the book of Psalms you feel compelled to say, "My, what a guy this David was. I'd love to have been his brother. I'd love to have carried his sword for him. I'd do anything for him."

The *soul* of David is one of the most attractive in all the Old Testament record. His *intellect* was first class—what an incredible, creative mind! His *emotions*—well, he might have been a little wild at times, but he vividly expressed emotions at both ends of the spectrum. So you might say he kept an overall balance. The *will?* What David set his heart and mind to do usually got done. Witness Goliath.

But his *body*. That was something else. When it came to the battle over bodily passions, David became extremely careless. And he paid for it very, very dearly. He won tremendous victories in the spirit. In his soul, he was irresistible—many people either loved him or stood in awe of him. But in his body, he was so woefully undisciplined that it wrecked his life and shattered his dreams.

That's why each one of us needs to watch all those areas in our lives.

We need to care for the spirit: memorize Scripture, attend worship services, spend time praising God, go to Bible studies, and maybe attend a top-rated Bible college. Do it all.

We need to care for the soul: keep the intellect clear, go as high as we can, write, read, have the best brain in the world; keep the emotions in balance; put the will under control of the Holy Spirit.

But we need to keep our body under subjection, too. That's where David faltered. He continually gave in to his bodily passions. When he found himself facing the temptation to sin with Bathsheba, he caved in all at once—with no hesitation. There was no inner resolve to resist, there was no inner voice to object. David's lustful passions shouted louder than his soul or spirit. So David listened. And David fell.

WAITING FOR GOD'S CHOICE

How crucial to put this area of our lives under the control and guidance of God's Holy Spirit. There's nothing more traumatic and nothing more sad than to see a Christian's marriage collapse in a great flood of bitterness, grief, and regret.

I get so desperate in urging Christian young men and women not to be stupid about sex and marriage. If there was ever a time they needed to consult their wise and loving Lord over any area, this is the time and this is the area. But so often they don't.

Young people need to be on their knees before God, asking Him if they should marry, when they should marry, and whom they should marry. They should pray earnestly for God to show them the things that will make a good marriage partner. It's not beautiful eyes that make a good wife, nor is it a good-looking, curvy body. It isn't eyelashes that go twiddle-twiddle (they'll fall out later on). Remember, no matter how much jogging you do or how much yogurt you eat, that body is still going to get wrinkled and worn out.

Man looks on the outward appearance but the Lord looks on the heart. Not that a good-looking girl or guy can't have a good-looking heart, too, but how carefully we should tread. You cannot trample the clear teaching of Scripture even in *one* area of your life without having it catch up with you sooner or later.

For instance, you know the Bible says not to marry unbelievers:

> *Do not be yoked together with unbelievers. For what do unrighteousness and wickedness have in common? Or what fellowship can light have with darkness? What harmony is there between Christ and Belial? What does a believer have in common with an unbeliever?* (2 Corinthians 6:14–15).

At one conference I was talking with a teenage girl whose parents had attended Bible college. As we talked I could see that they had already begun to compromise this very clear principle.

The girl said, "I want to be a missionary. I had such fun with the missionaries I met last week. I love missionaries. You're a great missionary. My folks support you. My big goal in life is to be a missionary in Latin America."

It seemed like she was headed in that direction. She spoke Spanish, had a good vocabulary, and loved Hispanic people. Our conversation ran down, so I pulled my usual with teenagers, "Have you got a boyfriend?"

"Sure!" she said with a smile.

"Is he a Christian?"

"Ah, hmmm, no."

"Drop him tonight," I said.

"Oh, no, I can't do that."

"Well," I said, "go on living in sin if you want."

"I don't live in sin," she said. "I love the Lord and want to be a missionary."

"Look," I said, "if you're dating a nonbeliever, forget about being a missionary. You're just playing games. It's a sin to go with a nonbeliever."

"What's so wrong about it?" she asked. "I'm not going to marry him."

"Then why are you going with him?"

"Oh, I'm not . . . ."

"You're playing around."

"No, no, I'm not playing around. I'm serious."

"Well, if you're serious, you're going to get married."

"No, no, I'm not going to get married."

"Well, then, you're playing around."

"No, I'm not playing around, it's just . . . ."

I said, "Now come on. Are you going to marry this man, or are you just going with him for kicks?"

She pulled all the typical excuses. I wrote them down.

Her: "I have no intention of marrying him."

Me: "Why all the kissing, then?"

Her: "All my Christian girlfriends are going with non-Christian guys."

Me: "Let them go through hell. But why do you want to go through hell?"

Her: "Besides, my boyfriend is under conviction. I'm witnessing to him."

Me: "Look, the best witness you could make would be to call him up tonight or at the latest tomorrow and say, 'Look, I've been thinking about our relationship and I see that I am in rebellion against the Word of God. I like you very much. But we can't go out any more, and certainly not go steady, because the Bible says I'm not supposed to marry an unbeliever. I don't want to put you on that I'm serious about you and want to marry you. It's against God's will. I'm in sin. I've asked the Lord to forgive me and I've got to break it up.' "

She said, "It would be a poor testimony to break up with him."

I said, "What's so poor about that testimony?"

She said, "Well, if I break with him just like that, he'll be so shocked that he'll turn against the Gospel."

I said, "Well, let him turn against the Gospel. But you've got to obey the Word of God. Besides, he won't turn."

And then she pulled the biggest excuse: "But my mother and I are praying for him." The mother had been telling my wife, Pat, this, too. I said, "Well, then your mother and you are both in sin."

"Praying for my boyfriend is a sin?" she asked.

"Yes," I said. "In the sense that you are praying it is. You can't ask God to bless something which He is against."

That mother—a Bible college graduate, supporter of missionaries—was slowly leading her daughter into disobedience and it was going to bring trouble for the girl's marriage. The mother should have said, "Honey, if you want to pray for what's-his-name, first you have to break up with him, then we'll pray that he will meet Christ."

A lot of evangelical Christians and their children are going through hell because they disobeyed God's command about not being yoked with unbelievers. In His grace, the Lord may save that unbelieving partner later on.

But I tell you, it isn't worth the years in between. And it isn't God's best.

Scripture clearly shows us that this tragedy haunts even God's choice people—young people with a heart for God. No one is immune. Even David destroyed his life at this point, the second most important decision in his life. He had a right relationship with God—that's the number one decision. But in number two—the woman (women) he married—he was careless.

Even though many men in that day took a number of wives, it wasn't what God wanted. David knew it. All he had to do was look over in Deuteronomy 17:17 to read it in black and white: "He must not take many wives, or his heart will be led astray." Here God is telling the people that the king He will raise up shouldn't have a lot of wives because they will turn his heart away from God. Since his teenage days David had known very well that he was going to be king. He also knew the law. But he chose to ignore this one little point. He couldn't get over his weakness for women.

If this had been a general command, rather than one addressed specifically to kings, David might have said, "Well, Lord, that law is for rabble—for the common people. If we didn't have these laws, our society would be a mess. But you know, I've been anointed king. I'll have the money to take on all kinds of wives." But David couldn't have missed it—the law specified *kings*. And he broke God's law. Outright.

THE GALATIANS 6 PRINCIPLE

What happened to David after that? He dried up. In Psalm 32:3–4 he admits:

93

A Man After God's Heart

When I kept silent,
   my bones wasted away
   through my groaning all day long.
For day and night
   your hand was heavy upon me;
my strength was sapped
   as in the heat of summer.

As long as David didn't confess his sins, he said, his bones dried up. Sexual immorality will dry up even the most excitable, talkative Christian. He may keep up a good front and mouth the right words, but his bones dry up. He's dead inside. That's because the Holy Spirit is grieved. And he will have no more joy until restitution and restoration have been done before the Lord, before the church, and before everybody else who was offended.

David was restored when he confessed—when he said to the Lord in the presence of the prophet, "I have sinned against the Lord." When he said that, the prophet immediately replied, "The Lord has forgiven your sins." Notice, though, what the prophet added:

But because by doing this you have made the
enemies of the Lord show utter contempt, the son
born to you will die (2 Samuel 12:14).

That's the Galatians 6 principle. There would be consequences to David's sin. You say, "Doesn't the Lord forgive? Doesn't the Lord restore?"

The answer is, "Yes, nevertheless . . . ." That's the Galatians 6 principle.

All the King's Horses, All the King's Men

You say, "But isn't the Lord understanding and compassionate and kind? Doesn't the Bible say God is love?

"Yes, nevertheless . . . ." Galatians 6:7–8 says:

> *Do not be deceived: God cannot be mocked. A man reaps what he sows. The one who sows to please his sinful nature, from that nature will reap destruction; the one who sows to please the Spirit, from the Spirit will reap eternal life.*

Whatever a man sows, he will reap. If he plants to please his own flesh, he will harvest a crop of death and destruction. If he plants to please the Spirit of God, he will harvest eternal life.

The Galatians 6 principle says you are responsible for what you have sown and for what you are sowing. Even though you confess your sins before God and find forgiveness, the forces have been set in motion. You will reap what you sow.

Even though the Lord had "put away" David's sin, the consequences would still come back to haunt him, like a bitter tide.

"Now therefore," the Lord told David, "the sword shall never depart from your own house, because you have despised me, and have taken the wife of Uriah the Hittite to be your wife."

David had sown in blood; he would reap bloodshed in his own family. David had sown in immorality; he would live to see a horrible harvest or immorality in his own home.

You remember this old nursery rhyme, don't you?

A Man After God's Heart

Humpty Dumpty sat on a wall,
Humpty Dumpty had a great fall.
All the king's horses,
And all the king's men,
Couldn't put Humpty together again.

Humpty Dumpty has some similarities to King David. The mythical egg-man started out in great shape. So did David. But the storybook character didn't quite have what it takes to sit on walls. David didn't have what it takes in the area of self-control. That area almost demolished him, put a brake on his upward career, brought a curse on his family, and created a fracture in the people of God.

David and Humpty Dumpty, however, have one considerable contrast. David had a King who put him back together again. Nevertheless, the cracks in the shell were there until the end. David never got to be what he could have been. We have no idea today, nor did David ever find out, what he missed out on because of his great fall.

But David was still David. The apple of God's eye was still the apple of God's eye. Broken and humbled before the One he had once served with burning zeal, the son of Jesse was ready to start back on the road he'd followed so fervently from his youth. The way he'd wandered so far away from. The way to God's heart.

And this is the beauty and hope and joy of serving our God. There is a way back. The road is still open through Christ. God's heart still yearns for our fellowship. Praise God that He is the God of the second chance . . . and the third . . . and three hundred and thirty-third.

All the King's Horses, All the King's Men

The psalmist says it:

If you, O LORD, kept a record of sins,
*   O Lord, who could stand?*
But with you there is forgiveness;
*   therefore you are feared*
(Psalm 130:3–4).

The storms would descend on this man David—fire storms of betrayal, persecution, grief, and disappointment. But David was ready now. He could look God in the face once again. He could write new songs for God's glory. And though the melody was now bittersweet, the theme was ever the same.

I wait for the LORD, my soul waits,
*   and in his word I put my hope.*
My soul waits for the Lord
*   more than watchmen for the morning,*
*   more than watchmen wait for the morning*
O Israel, put your hope in the LORD . . .
(Psalm 130:5–7).

Chapter 6

"I Have Called You Friends"

THE MAN AFTER GOD'S HEART had a heart for men.

The son of Jesse stands strong and tall in the inspired record as a true and loyal friend. It makes sense, doesn't it?

Can a man call himself the friend of God if he refuses friendship to men? If the Creator longs after the rebellious creature formed in His own image, can the one who walks with God hold himself aloof? It should not be considered extraordinary that the man who evidenced such a profound commitment to his God was a man who formed deep commitments to men.

THE LONGING FOR FRIENDSHIP

Knowing my own heart, I am convinced that all men dream of deep friendship with either one man or a small group of men. Something inside man longs for a soul-brother—a brother he would be willing to die for. I believe God wove such a desire into the innermost fabric of our beings. I can't speak for women, but I'm confident I speak for many, many

99

men. There is that secret dream that if the circumstances demanded it, in spite of human selfishness and sinfulness, the man would surrender his life for a buddy.

Of course, this does not at all take away from the friendship of a man and his wife. My best friend in all the world is my wife, Pat. I wouldn't trade her friendship for that of anyone else. Augustine once observed that when God saw Adam was lonely, He didn't create ten friends, but one wife. Yet, in spite of the fact that your wife is the closest of all human companions, a restless something under a man's skin cries out for the trust and friendship of another man or men. Someone with whom he can do exploits. Someone to help him fight the world. Someone to stick it out—thick or thin, win or lose.

Maybe that's what makes the David and Jonathan story hit a man at gut level. Maybe that's what makes that portion of God's Word so attractive and compelling. Civilizations have grown and crumbled away, awesome armies have marched and armies have fallen, once-mighty kings, commanders, and self-proclaimed emperors lie forgotten in ancient mud . . . but the friendship of David and Jonathan— after four thousand years—goes on winning hearts and conquering men.

What a remarkable friendship! Not that Jonathan was David's only friend, but these men loved each other until death.

THE EXAMPLE OF FRIENDSHIP

We've already relived that historic day when the youngest son of the Bethlehemite rancher toppled Goliath with a single stone and led the hordes of Israel to rout the menacing Philistines. But the Goliath story has a number of subplots. One of the most noteworthy friendships of all time began that very day.

> *After David had finished talking with Saul, Jonathan became one in spirit with David, and he loved him as himself. From that day Saul kept David with him and would not let him return to his father's house. . . . Jonathan took off the robe he was wearing and gave it to David, along with his tunic, and even his sword, his bow and his belt* (1 Samuel 18:1–2, 4).

These were men who by all rights should have been bitter rivals. Both had a claim to the throne of Israel, Jonathan by birth and David by the anointing of Samuel. In those days you didn't try to undercut your political rivals by bugging their offices or tapping their telephones or launching a smear campaign against them. You simply killed them. By all means—by any means.

But not David and Jonathan. There wasn't an ounce of competition between them. After Jonathan saw David defeat the enemy's champion, Saul's son felt his soul knit to the son of Jesse. It was an immediate, inseparable bond. Jonathan loved David as himself.

Then the Israelite prince did something totally unexpected—even incredible. In front of his father the king, in front of the general of the armies, in front of all Israel, Jonathan removed his royal garments, unbuckled his sword and the trappings identifying him as heir to the throne, and put them all at the feet of the teenage shepherd.

Do you realize the implications of such an act? Perhaps you're thinking, "Hmm. Nice gesture. He gave his buddy a new suit. So what?"

Try to picture yourself in the following situation. Imagine you're visiting London and have the opportunity to tour Buckingham Palace. As you follow the guided tour through all the gilded rooms you are pleasantly surprised to see the entire royal family in all their regalia standing in one of the large halls. "Hey!" you say. "I didn't know *this* came with the tour."

Your guide pauses, allowing everyone to drink it all in. As you're fishing in your pack for your pocket camera, you notice Prince Charles step forward and whisper something to one of the stone-faced honor guards. Suddenly the soldier summons you to come and kneel before the royal family. Stunned beyond words, you leave your open-mouthed tour group and wobble your way over to their highnesses.

As you kneel, the Prince of Wales dramatically strides forward, studies you for a moment, then whisks off his regal robe and wraps it across your shoulders. Before you can catch your breath, he slips his royal signet ring on your finger, places his golden scepter in your right hand, and sets his ancient crown on your head. He then announces that he has given up all rights to the throne and proclaims *you* will be the next British king or queen!

Can you visualize it? Then perhaps you can begin to understand the shock-waves rippling through the ranks of Israel following Jonathan's symbolic act.

"I Have Called You Friends"

"David, my friend," Jonathan was saying, "here's my promise to you. Not even the throne will come between us!"

Instead of competing with one another, it seems they were constantly trying to promote one another. This is what friendship is all about. When a man loves another man or a woman loves another woman in such a way that they promote each other instead of themselves—this is a mark of the genuine article . . . real friendship.

THE LOYALTY OF FRIENDSHIP

The friendship of David and Jonathan grew up in the sunshine of a victory celebration. It grew strong under the dark skies of royal jealousy and political intrigue as the smile of Saul's favor curled into the sneer of suspicion. It didn't take long.

When the men were returning home after David had killed the Philistine, the women came out from all the towns of Israel to meet King Saul with singing and dancing, with joyful songs and with tambourines and lutes. As they danced, they sang:

"Saul has slain his thousands,
    and David his tens of thousands."

Saul was very angry; this refrain galled him. "They have credited David with tens of thousands," he thought, "but me with only thousands. What more can he get but the kingdom?" And from that time on Saul kept a jealous eye on David (1 Samuel 18:6–9).

A Man After God's Heart

The word went out. David, the instant hero, was a marked man. He didn't need his face on a "wanted" poster in all the post offices. The word just got around: Saul wanted to retire David—permanently. And anyone in Israel who wanted to gain an immediate five-level raise in his civil service rating without taking the exam knew what he had to do. David may as well have embroidered a target on the back of his coat.

But then . . . enter Jonathan. Knowing all too well the murderous level of his father's envy, the king's son scooped all his available courage and stepped up to bat for his new friend.

> *Jonathan spoke well of David to Saul his father and said to him, "Let not the king do wrong to his servant David; he has not wronged you, and what he has done has benefited you greatly"*
> (1 Samuel 19:4).

Finding his father in one of those rare listening moods, the crown prince rehearsed David's valorous deeds on the nation's behalf. "Remember how you felt that day when David shut Goliath's big mouth—remember that, Dad? Hey—and remember how we took off after those Philistines and how they scattered like quail before the bowman? Remember how the wine flowed and how we laughed and danced and sang?

"Remember? And now you're trying to spill the blood of your servant David? The man who sings like an angel and strums his harp to heal your jangled nerves? Think about it, Dad. It doesn't add up. It doesn't make sense."

"I Have Called You Friends"

So Saul remembered and repented—for a while. But jealous kings have short memories when it comes to recalling their rivals' redeeming features. After a brief respite, Saul was at it again. This time when Jonathan intervened, it nearly cost him his life.

> *Saul's anger flared up at Jonathan and he said to him, "You son of a perverse and rebellious woman! Don't I know that you have sided with the son of Jesse to your own shame and to the shame of the mother who bore you? As long as the son of Jesse lives on this earth, neither you nor your kingdom will be established. Now send and bring him to me, for he must die!"* (1 Samuel 20:30–31).

When Jonathan argued the point further, Saul hurled his spear at him and would have killed his own son if Jonathan had not been quick to dodge. As far as his friend David was concerned, Jonathan did not count his own life precious. He was fully willing to defend the son of Jesse before anyone—even to the point of death.

These two men were totally committed to each other, vowing that whoever survived and came out on top would protect the other's descendants. Jonathan, however, didn't have much doubt as to who would be number one. Once when David was hiding in the forest the son of Saul sought his friend to encourage him and "strengthen his hand in the Lord."

> *"Don't be afraid," he said. "My father Saul will not lay a hand on you. You will be king over*

A Man After God's Heart

Israel, and I will be second to you. Even my father Saul knows this" (1 Samuel 23:17).

Jonathan was saying, "David, it's going to be good. You and me. You'll be king and I'll stand at your right hand—no matter what. Israel will blossom, David. Can't you just see it?"

Jonathan had a dream. In his spirit he could see the beginnings of David's glory—a mighty and eternal dynasty. And Jonathan would not let his own ego or personal aspirations stand in the way of that dream's fulfillment. David would reign. Jonathan would be happy and content to surrender his own rights and stand at the side of God's chosen king. Willing to be number two. Willing to let God exalt as He would.

How beautiful it would be if there were more of this in the Body of Christ. Friendships unthreatened by overblown egos. Friendships unafraid of commitment. Friendships unshaken by pressure, hardship, or sudden turn of events. Friendships that speak the same words face to face or ten thousand miles apart.

When most of us speak of friendship or "fellowship," we're talking about something different than the bond that David and Jonathan enjoyed. We draw invisible lines within our friendships and say, "This far and no further. I will be your friend . . . as long as it doesn't cost me very much. I will be your friend . . . as long as it doesn't involve a heavy commitment. I will be your friend . . . until distance, promotion, or pressing activities draw us apart. I will be your friend . . . as long as it's convenient . . . as long as it doesn't embarrass me or cramp my style . . . as long as it brings me personal pleasure. Beyond that, forget it."

We live in an age that says, "You only go around once in life, buddy, so grab all you can. Make a friend, marry a wife, raise a family until it looks like they're beginning to impede your progress, then—ditch them. Write them off. After all, you've got to watch out for old number one. So use anybody you must to get what you want. Then when they get in your way, kiss them good-bye."

That's the kind of world we live in. A world that's haughty and proud on the outside but crushed with loneliness and longing inside. God created within us the need for commitment and security in our relationships; in our relationship with God, in our relationship with family, and in our relationship with friends. To the point we remain true to our own commitments, to the point we are willing to sacrifice our own best interests to promote and build in other lives—to that point—we find our deepest longings fulfilled.

Jonathan and David vowed to care for one another's families if something should happen to one of them. Jonathan could say, "Hey, Dave, if you go before I do, don't worry about your family. I'll take care of them like they were my own. So put it out of your mind, buddy. You can count on it." And David could say the same.

How about you? What if your "best friend" died today? What would you do? Send his wife a $2 sympathy card? Send a bunch of flowers that'll wilt in three days? Stop in for five minutes every six months to give your regards? What does friendship really mean to you? I fear that many of us really shine when it comes to loving "with words or tongue" but slip out the back door when it comes to living "with actions and in truth" (1 John 3:18).

How smoothly and glibly the words roll off our tongues. "I love you, brother. I love you, sister." "I'll be praying for you." "I enjoy your fellowship." Really? Examine your words of "love and commitment" very carefully. God does. One day we will stand before the throne of our Jesus Christ to "give account . . . for every careless word" we have spoken (Matthew 12:36).

What kind of friend are you?

THE TEAMWORK OF FRIENDSHIP

During the course of my world-wide evangelistic ministry the Lord has privileged me to work with a team of men and women. We're a bunch of sinners, saved by the grace of God, but we still live for each other and pray daily for each other.

Some team members live thousands of miles away in Miami. Some live many thousands of miles further away in Argentina. Others live in Guatemala, still others in England. Yet when we come together we hug each other—like a typical bunch of Latinos—and enjoy working together as if it had been only a few weeks' separation.

It's a great thing when a group of people can work together like that. I have friends I don't see for months, but the moment we're together it's like we just had dinner together last Tuesday. There's an immediate sense of closeness. David and Jonathan had such a friendship. And you know, if we were more like Jesus Christ, controlled by His indwelling presence, we would be more and more like that to more and more people. Not exclusively with one or two or three, but able to embrace more people.

Although you can't be close to everybody, because time doesn't allow it, your attitude can be warm and loving and kind. How I long to be that kind of person! The Lord Jesus can develop this in us because He lives within us, as believers, and He was and is the perfect Friend. Proverbs 18:24 states: "A man of many companions may come to ruin, but there is a friend who sticks closer than a brother." Down through the ages, the true followers of Jesus have found those words eminently true of their Master. Do you know Him as your Friend?

Decision magazine, published by the Billy Graham Association, once featured a story about two single missionary men in Africa during the time of the Simba rebellion. At that particular time, admitting American citizenship was tantamount to signing your own death warrant. One of these two missionaries was British and he could easily have saved himself from an attacking mob by flashing his British passport. But, instead, he chose to stick by the American missionary who was threatened with death. The British missionary had his passport and successfully passed as American. When the Simbas came to bludgeon the American to death, the British man threw himself on his friend and was killed.

Friendship. It's more than sentiment. It's more than exchanging Christmas cards and baby pictures. Jesus said, "Greater love has no one than this, that he lay down his life for his friends" (John 15:13). Are you that kind of friend? It can happen only through Him.

A Man After God's Heart

THE GRIEF OF FRIENDSHIP

The common reaction to the dismay and destruction of our enemies is one of suppressed jubilation, if not open celebration. You recognize the need to look properly sober on the outside but it's hard to keep the corners of your mouth from a slight upward bend. Inside you're thinking, "Oh boy, did he get his. Serves him right."

If anyone was entitled to a little smug satisfaction on the death of Saul, it would have to be David. Hunted and hounded by the jealous king for years on end, David would have had ample time to plan his victory celebration as he ran from one cave, cavern, or hole in the ground to another.

Because of Saul, David was forced to flee for his life, endure separation from friends and family, survive in a hostile wilderness, and make a pact with his sworn enemies. How many nights had he shivered in the open air, driven from shelter, wondering which breath would be his last because of Saul's relentless, pursuing army? How many tears of loneliness, exhaustion, and despair had he shed alone in the wilds or in a damp cave in fear of Saul's sword?

So when the news of Saul's destruction dropped in David's lap, was it any wonder that he . . . broke down and wept? Amazing! The least one might have expected would be a mixed reaction, for both Saul *and Jonathan* had met violent death at the hands of the Philistines. But David didn't pick and choose. He wept for both men.

> *Then David and all the men with him took hold of their clothes and tore them. They mourned and wept and fasted till evening for Saul and his son*

110

"I Have Called You Friends"

Jonathan, and for the army of the LORD and the house of Israel, because they had fallen by the sword (2 Samuel 1:11–12).

Notice this. Remember who Saul was. Saul was David's enemy to the death, but Saul was the king. And the son of Jesse had an awe, respect, and loyalty for the anointed of God, whoever or whatever he may have been.

When David received the news in Ziklag, he could have easily replied with justified sarcasm, "Yeah, long live the king. I am the king!"

But David wept.

I wonder how many people who so enthusiastically campaigned for a popular candidate later weep for him if he falls. We are such sometime friends. We'll stick with a man if he's a winner, but the moment he's in trouble we become candidates for an Olympic Gold Medal in backpedaling. We're all ready to support the next one who steps in the limelight. Let's face it, in our carnal human nature we're basically fickle and disloyal.

But not David. I'm convinced that loyalty of heart toward others is one of the things we must ask God to give us. Not only loyalty for your husband or wife—this is already in bad shape in our society, where at the slightest provocation people opt for "no-fault" divorce—but loyalty for friends, for employers, for others in the Body of Christ.

Note carefully David's actions in the first few chapters of 2 Samuel. It would have been a natural response if David had placed the crown of Saul on his own head and proclaimed himself king of all Israel. Had he not been

111

anointed of Samuel? But he didn't do that. After compos-
ing a tender memorial dirge for Saul and Jonathan, the son
of Jesse got down on his knees.

> *In the course of time, David inquired of the* LORD.
> *"Shall I go up to one of the towns of Judah?"*
> *The* LORD *said, "Go up."*
> *David asked, "Where shall I go?"*
> *"To Hebron," the* LORD *answered.*
> *So David went up there with his two wives . . .*
> (2 Samuel 2:1–2).

Instead of jumping on his own bandwagon and setting
up campaign headquarters throughout Israel and Judah,
David simply fell back on his Lord.

"Okay Lord, what now? Which way? I'm ready to roll
or I'm ready to wait. It's up to you."

KINDNESS OF FRIENDSHIP

Even years later, David had not forgotten his devotion
to Jonathan and Saul when he inquired, "Is there anyone
still left of the house of Saul to whom I can show kindness
for Jonathan's sake?" (2 Samuel 9:1).

When told there was one, Jonathan's son
Mephibosheth who was crippled in both feet, David
brought him into his own royal house and treated him as one
of the king's sons. After all those years, David remembered
the promise he had made to Jonathan, his friend. And this
was something more than a passive observance of his vow,
because David actually had to search for Mephibosheth,
since the son of Jonathan had been in hiding.

To me, another very touching reflection of David's loyalty is that, although he brought Mephibosheth to the palace for Jonathan's sake, yet again and again he referred to the crippled man's grandfather, Saul. Years had elapsed, yet David remembered the time when, in the heat of the battle, he'd had Saul at his mercy. David had crept up behind Saul in a cave and snipped off a piece of his coat.

When they were back outside, David called to him, "Hey, Saul, look what I have." And Saul, in a moment of fake repentance, had said, "Oh, David my son, is that your voice? When you become king, swear to me that you will be merciful to my descendants."

In those days, when one king fell, the next king felt obliged to murder the rest of the family so no one would rise up against him. Yet David promised Saul he wouldn't do that. Once firmly established in his kingdom, David remembered the words of his vow to the dead man and told the crippled grandson of Saul, "For the sake of your grandfather and your father, you are going to eat at my table like a prince for the rest of your days." Mephibosheth was astounded. "I'm just a crippled dog. And you want me to sit at your table?"

In many communist countries over the past generation, the victims of political "purges" became "nonpersons." Not only were they executed and buried in unmarked graves, their names were methodically erased from all the history books in the land. Their faces disappeared from old photographs. Old clippings were destroyed. It became as if they'd never existed at all. Mephibosheth must have felt like that.

A Man After God's Heart

"Hey, what are you doing, King David? Who am I? I'm a nothing—a nobody—a nonperson. Why should I look on the face of the king? Why should I eat bread with the king's sons?"

And David told him, "Mephibosheth, it's not because of anything great or small which you've done or which you've failed to do. I accept you because of your father. I accept you because I promised your grandfather. Enter now into the king's house and enjoy all the provisions on my table. You shall be as my son."

What a picture of what God the Father does for you and me. We enter into the Kingdom because of Another. We could never earn the right at all. We sit at the King's table and eat the King's food on the merit of our relationship to Another. We are accepted in the Beloved. Crippled, broken "nonpersons" in every sense of the word, He sought us out and called us to Himself. All we had to do was acknowledge His gracious invitation and accept His provision.

Mephibosheth could have rejected David's offer. He could have clung to his own poverty, misery, and obscurity, spitting on the king's messenger and spurning the king's message. And he would have been a fool.

Have *you* accepted *your* King's astounding offer of pardon and provision? Have you taken time today to thank your Lord for seating a crippled soul like *you* at the table of the King?

> *How great is the love the Father has lavished*
> *on us, that we should be called children of God!*
> (1 John 3:1).

"I Have Called You Friends"

PERVERSION OF FRIENDSHIP

What the world cannot understand, it either dismisses or perverts. David's relationship with Jonathan was so pure, so unselfish, so deep, and so strong that people who have rejected God cannot believe it. "There must have been ulterior motives," they reason in their dark minds. "They must have had a homosexual relationship."

That incredibly twisted idea, so false in every way, nevertheless has become commonplace in these days of national decline. Because the mind apart from Jesus Christ cannot fathom the concept of a true, selfless, Christlike friendship, it bends and distorts the truth of Scripture to fit its own warped philosophies. Militant homosexuals even have the audacity to use the relationship of Jonathan and David as a proof-text to justify all sorts of behavior.

I am astonished at how many Christians I've met who do not seem to have any biblical convictions about the goodness of a pure friendship or about the wrongness of homosexual or lesbian activity.

Even at Bible conferences, people have come up to my wife and me and said, "Well, there's nothing in the Bible about homosexuality." They must have an abridged edition or haven't read it carefully. There's enough in the Bible on this subject to build an airtight case against this and every other sexual sin.

Scripture is very clear that adultery is a serious violation of God's holy standards. It's also very clear that sex outside of marriage, whether heterosexual or homosexual or incestuous, is sinful.

115

A Man After God's Heart

Let's look at what the Bible specifically says about homosexual activity. Take time to read this passage very carefully. Don't skim—it's too important.

The wrath of God is being revealed from heaven against all the godlessness and wickedness of men who suppress the truth by their wickedness, since what may be known about God is plain to them, because God has made it plain to them. For since the creation of the world God's invisible qualities—his eternal power and divine nature— have been clearly seen, being understood from what has been made, so that men are without excuse.

For although they knew God, they neither glorified him as God nor gave thanks to him, but their thinking became futile and their foolish hearts were darkened. Although they claimed to be wise, they became fools and exchanged the glory of the immortal God for images made to look like mortal man and birds and animals and reptiles.

Therefore God gave them over in the sinful desires of their hearts to sexual impurity for the degrading of their bodies with one another. They exchanged the truth of God for a lie, and worshiped and served created things rather than the Creator—who is forever praised. Amen.

Because of this, God gave them over to shameful lusts. Even their women exchanged natural relations for unnatural ones. In the same way the men also abandoned natural relations with women and were inflamed with lust for one another. Men committed indecent acts with other men, and received in themselves the due penalty for their perversion.

Furthermore, since they did not think it worthwhile to retain the knowledge of God, he gave them over to a depraved mind, to do what ought not to be done (Romans 1:18–28).

In this powerful portion of Scripture, we're told that the final test of a homosexually active man or woman who refuses to repent is God giving him or her over to a depraved mind. *The Living Bible* paraphrases this well:

When they gave God up and would not even acknowledge him, God gave them up to doing everything their evil minds could think of. (Romans 1:28 TLB)

People who indulge in this sin are exchanging God's truth for a lie. It's a damnable trade—and they know it. They know exactly what they are doing. Nature itself teaches what is right, but they switch it around to their own destruction.

Like those who practice heterosexual sin, homosexuals worship the creature rather than the Creator. They worship themselves, actually. They love to look at their own bodies. Therefore God says to them, "You are turning My truth into a lie. You are worshiping your own body instead of Me—so go ahead and go all the way. If you've stubbornly set your mind in that direction, I'm not going to stop you. I'll let you see how it will be to serve your own depraved mind rather than serving your God."

Remember, this isn't easy for God. He loves lost men and women. He sent His Son to suffer and die for our sins such as these. But if a man or woman deliberately spurns that offer, trampling it underfoot, God will not violate that person's will. Each man or woman must choose whom he or she will serve.

One hears fantastic, incredible arguments today. To some, they're so very reasonable. This is evidence of a depraved mind—so hardened against God that it has ceased to be ashamed of its own corruption. At least in the old days people were hypocritical.

How much better to be a hypocrite and hide in the closet than to be a shameless person who openly flaunts immorality in the name of "personal rights" or "religious freedom." At least a hypocrite, by his very hypocrisy, is saying, "Listen man, I'm a pervert, but I'm not going to talk about it."

But the person who throws restraint aside, stands forward and says, "Gay is fun, gay is right, God loves gays . . . ." God releases such people to serve their own depravity. And what a horrible tyrant to serve. Throw that door wide open and every imaginable sorrow stakes a claim on what's left of that mind. We've seen the same thing with the heterosexual revolution this past generation, as well.

One of the former proponents of spouse swapping, group sex, trial marriage, and other sexual experiments, George Leonard, admits, "What I have learned is that there are no games without rules." People can try to break

God's moral laws, but they always will have to pay the consequences.

> *"Do you not know," says the apostle Paul, "that the wicked will not inherit the kingdom of God? Do not be deceived: Neither the sexually immoral nor idolaters nor adulterers nor male prostitutes nor homosexual offenders nor thieves nor the greedy nor drunkards nor slanderers nor swindlers will inherit the kingdom of God"* (1 Corinthians 6:9–10).

We need to learn those Scriptures—commit them to memory—be alert. Not for the purpose of arguing but simply to be ready to use the Word of God in the power of the Holy Spirit.

Even in the midst of an age such as ours, this sort of loyal, abiding love is possible through the One who said, "Never will I leave you; never will I forsake you" (Hebrews 13:5).

Because Jesus Christ called us to be His friends, we can experience the privilege of demonstrating true friendship to an incredulous, sin-weary world.

Chapter 7

David Had a Dream

SOMETIMES ALL IT TAKES is a little storm. No thundering, sky-splitting tempest or howling hurricane—just a few dark clouds, a stiff breeze. And all the walls come crashing down.

Some people fall into a thousand pieces because of little things—the small hurts and tragedies life regularly throws in the path of humankind.

But David withstood huge, catastrophic storms and terrible upheavals in his lifetime. How did he do it? How can you and I learn to face the inevitable major crises of life? David, for all his emotional ups and downs, had God-given perspective. David learned to look at situations—even heartbreaks—from God's point of view. He became great in the eyes of God and men because he sought God's perspective on the course of his nation and on history. Combined with a caring heart, this perspective reached out into a worldwide vision for serving the people of God.

A Man After God's Heart

These twin elements—an historical perspective and a worldwide vision—will lend stability to any life. The person who develops and maintains these qualities is not likely to fall victim to pressing circumstances and little storms. Although these may occur in his life, they will not destroy him because he is able to perceive a larger picture than the little box of his own pain and perplexity. He sees his life in the balance of history. Many people may encounter a little problem in their church, but they don't throw up their hands and think the world is at its end if they have the Bible's historical perspective.

Bombs explode in the Jerusalem marketplace and terrorists threaten New York, but the person with perception isn't panicked into thinking he's missed the Second Coming. In reading his Bible he realizes that many of the things happening today have happened before.

The most important thing is learning how to view both worldwide and personal crises and, further, learning how to handle them. The Christian asks, "How did the old brethren handle these things? I want to face them the same way. I want to learn from their mistakes and their victories and their faith" (see Hebrews 13:7).

Even though he didn't have television, newspapers, Rand-McNally maps, jet airplanes, or *Time* magazine, David had an historical perspective.

Why do the nations conspire
and the peoples plot in vain?
The kings of the earth take their stand

> *and the rulers gather together*
> *against the L*ORD
> *and against his Anointed One.*
> *"Let us break their chains," they say,*
> *"and throw off their fetters."*
>
> *The One enthroned in heavens laughs;*
> *the Lord scoffs at them.*
> *Then he rebukes them in his anger*
> *and terrifies them in his wrath, saying,*
> *"I have installed my King*
> *on Zion, my holy hill."*
>
> *I will proclaim the decree of the L*ORD*:*
>
> *He said to me, "You are my Son;*
> *today I have become your Father.*
> *Ask of Me,*
> *and I will make the nations your inheritance,*
> *the ends of the earth your possession.*
> *You will rule them with an iron scepter;*
> *you will dash them to pieces like*
> *pottery"* (Psalm 2:1–9).

Note especially those last verses. We all know that this refers in part to Jesus Christ as the Messiah. But the exciting thing is this: Even though David didn't have instant knowledge about events taking place around the world, as we do, he had a worldwide vision and an historical perspective. He was able to step back and evaluate the nations according to their relationship with God.

A Man After God's Heart

David asks, "Why are the nations in such an uproar? Why do they engage in these international conferences against the Lord and His Anointed? What do they expect to accomplish?" The nations may plot their strategies, they may issue their ultimatums regarding Jesus Christ and His Gospel, but God will simply laugh at them. He will scoff at them. He will look down at them and say, "Those little finite beings down there . . . they think they're going to put Me down. They think they're going to destroy the King. They must be joking, but they're not. So because they are not, I'm going to step all over them—I'm going to demolish them like a clay jar smashed on a rock."

The nations are still in an uproar today. You read of revolutions and wars, upheaval in the former Soviet Union, tension in the Arab world, and uncertainty in the Western world. But the Christian who has long-range historical perspective and worldwide vision doesn't panic like the non-Christian. He knows what's behind it all. And he is aware that God knows.

Notice how David wraps up that psalm:

Therefore, you kings, be wise;
    be warned, you rulers of the earth.
Serve the LORD with fear
    and rejoice with trembling.
Kiss the Son, lest he be angry
    and you be destroyed in your way,
for his wrath can flare up in a moment.
    Blessed are all who take refuge in him
(2:10–12).

David Had a Dream

Even though David had a realistic perspective on how God viewed the warring nations, he also had a passion for those who didn't know his Lord. He wanted them to worship God, too.

I was eighteen years old in Argentina when I began to really give my life over to the Lord. I attended a very small local church—only about 120 to 130 could squeeze into the chapel. Sometimes in the summer they opened the windows and those who couldn't fit inside would stand outside under the windows to listen.

It was a good place for a teenager to be because they encouraged the young men to preach and gave us ample opportunity to practice. The elders would gather around afterwards and give us tips on how to improve our sermoncraft, delivery, and so on. But through my mother and some friends who prayed with me, I started to look beyond our little church in Argentina.

Psalm 22 began to get in my blood.

All the ends of the earth
*   will remember and turn to the* LORD,
and all the families of the nations
*   will bow down before him,*
for dominion belongs to the LORD,
*   and he rules over the nations.*

All the rich of the earth will feast and worship;
*   all who go down to the dust will*
*   kneel before him—*
those who cannot keep themselves alive.

A Man After God's Heart

Posterity will serve him;
future generations will be told about
the Lord.
They will proclaim his righteousness
to a people yet unborn—
for he has done it
(verses 27–31).

In this psalm, David speaks of "the ends of the earth." Remember that in those days they didn't have TV, supersonic transport, or satellite mapping. Yet David had a worldwide vision. Why? Because he'd been in the presence of God. He'd been taught by the Lord. Even though he didn't have a fraction of the scriptures we have today, David had enough to receive instruction from God. He saw that all the families of the nations would worship before the Lord.

A GLOBAL PERSPECTIVE

Herein lies an important key to maturity: Those who are really serious about the Lord's service ask Him for global vision and an historical, biblical perspective.

When I read the paper, I don't get hung up on the political details of everything, but I try to see the hand of God in the movements of nations. When there is a revolution in some country, I try not to think of it as, "Oh well, another egomaniac gone berserk. Shot the king. Who's in charge now?" Instead, I try to ask myself, "Now what's God trying to do in that country? How will this affect the missionary effort in that area?" And even though I may have never met a person from that country in my life, I know I can pray for that nation.

Anyone who really gets involved in understanding God's worldwide activity cannot be content to simply sit back and think of his own pleasure. He's going to get a passion and a vision for the lost. David did—and that was thousands of years ago!

My mother was a woman with global perspective. When I was a teenager, she kept saying, "There are so many millions of people who haven't heard about Jesus Christ. You've got to get out there, Luis. Let's have Sunday school. Let's have children's meetings. Start new churches." So we began to serve the Lord teaching children and then young people. We'd have all-night prayer meetings, and would often get up at 5:00 A.M. to study the Bible at other times. She passed her vision on to me.

VISION COMING TO PASS

In my late teens and early twenties the Lord began to build on that vision, giving me the intense desire to see not only the area around my home evangelized, but the whole city. Then, thanks to a missionary, that vision grew still larger and I began to think of the entire country of Argentina. Then the continent of Latin America. As my friends and I would pray, we asked the Lord to let us see three nations in our continent become fifty-one percent truly born-again evangelical Christian.

When we started praying it seemed like such a wild dream. But it's coming about, in God's time. One nation already is more than 30 percent converted. We're seeing

God bring tremendous fruit in many other parts of the world, as well.

Whenever I speak at conferences or camps and get together with teenagers who love the Lord Jesus, I often wonder if they have passion in their souls for people who don't know Christ. Every one of us will have it if we spend time in the presence of the Lord.

When I was eighteen, the Lord began to bring into my mind the idea of working to evangelize millions of people through radio, television, and literature. But until I was thirty-two, even though the Lord had opportunities for me here and there, nothing very big seemed to break.

Those years seemed to last forever. We worked, we expected, we prayed, we planned. I filled notebooks with notes, charts, ideas, and plans. Sometimes it seemed the answer would never come. Yet in my soul, I knew God was bringing it about. I didn't know how. My mother was a widow and we were extremely poor. For years, I had to support my five sisters, my brother, and mother. Yet I knew that someday, somehow, God would do it. For twelve years I dreamed, prayed, planned, prepared notes . . . and waited. When God inspires a vision, we can know He'll make it happen.

David had a dream, I believe, that he would see the day when the earth would be filled with the glory of God as the waters cover the sea.

EVEN BEFORE KINGS

When I was eighteen I used to pray secretly, "Lord Jesus, use me to evangelize. Use me not only with children"—that's what I was doing at the time and there's nothing better to begin with than children—"not only with young people and adults, but Lord, grant me the privilege to witness for You before presidents, kings, and governors."

I didn't tell a soul about this prayer, because others would have thought I was big-headed. But in my heart I longed and prayed for this privilege. I said, "Lord Jesus, even if they kill me, I will tell them about the Gospel."

God has granted me the fulfillment of some of the grandest of these dreams. I've had repeated opportunities to sit before presidents, talking to them about the Lord Jesus as openly as I'd talk to any child out at a Bible camp. Of course, I treat them with more protocol, but it's the same Gospel.

Once the Lord opened a door for me to talk with the president of a South American republic at a Presidential Breakfast. Before it began, he inquired, "Palau, what are you going to talk about so I can think about a response?"

"Mr. President," I said, "I'm going to talk about the crises of the spirit."

"Crises!" the president frowned. "Let *me* tell you about crises!"

There I was, an evangelist, sitting beside the president whom I'd met only a few minutes earlier. And yet there he was openly sharing deep crises in his personal life.

As he talked, I thought to myself, "I can't believe it, Lord. This isn't some college student opening up here—this is the president of the republic pouring out his story, asking for counsel!"

Earlier, our team had gone to a Central American country and asked for an interview with the president. We were granted a ten-minute time slot but the president kept us for forty-five! As the conversation went on and became more personal, the president asked all his aides to leave the room. Only the president, two team members, and I remained. The president spoke slowly, with great feeling.

"The only answer to the problems of this country," he said, "is the message you people proclaim. There is no other option that will save our nation."

"That's what we feel is our contribution to the nation, Mr. President," I said. "We want to bring as many people as possible to a born-again experience with Christ. Then they'll be better citizens, and the nations will be a better place."

"I know it," he said. "I'm with you."

Do you know what happened? Two years later we went back to the western states of that nation. We drove into the number two city of the country and all over the city found posters that read, "The government invites you to come hear Luis Palau." My driver almost went in the ditch!

These posters had been printed on the government presses and put up by municipal workers at night—without a penny's cost to us. About 5,000 posters—put up because of a president's order to his public relations people. Because a president wanted his people to hear about Jesus Christ.

One night, as we came out of one of the crusade meetings, I noticed what I thought was a suspicious-looking character watching me in the shadows from the stadium. I said to those with me, "Watch out for that man—the one who's heading straight for his car. He's obviously in a hurry. Keep an eye on him."

When we got to our hotel, there he was in the shadows again out on the sidewalk. I ran to the room, rousted the other team members, and they went down and grabbed him.

"What do you want?" they demanded.

"The president sent me here!" the man said. This man was an assistant to the president for tourism. "If Mr. Palau needs a car, let me know," he said. "We also want to put him up in a decent hotel instead of this cheap place. We've also opened the northern borders so people can come in without papers to hear Mr. Palau's message. And he can come and evangelize any time he wants."

God just opened up the door. We hadn't even dared ask Him for something like that. You say, "All of this for an Argentine evangelist? How did it happen?" I believe it began to happen in my eighteenth year when I really started praying that whole nations would hear the Good News. I asked the Lord to do it. And the Lord has and *will yet* do it. Again and again.

SHINE WHERE YOU ARE

Luke 16:10 says, "Whoever can be trusted with very little can also be trusted with much." So first, you shine where you are—reach everyone you can in your own "Jerusalem." Put your whole heart into whatever job the Lord has put into your hands to do, no matter how mundane or trivial it may seem (Colossians 3:23).

When David was a shepherd, he protected his sheep to the best of his ability. And as a soldier, he served King Saul as a faithful and loyal servant. He knew he was anointed by God as future king, but he patiently waited for

God's timing. Pray big prayers—dream great dreams before your Father.

This doesn't mean you must be perfect before the Lord will use you. Just ask my wife if I'm perfect . . . she'll tell you! Luke 16:10 does mean, however, that if you are trustworthy according to the light you have, if you are obedient to what the Lord lays before you each day, He will open another door of opportunity, and another. And yet another. The only limitations to our service in the kingdom are the ones we impose, either by faithlessness or by lack of holiness or disobedience. Otherwise, any one of us could be used by God with mighty power.

A certain country of South America persecuted and killed Christians for years. Their terrorism was particularly heavy in the early 1960s, when my wife and I and our two small sons moved there as missionaries. At that time, that nation had almost no missionaries—they hadn't returned after the violence that killed a quarter of a million people, including 135 preachers of the Gospel. Eighty-five chapels were bombed in those dark days.

It was tough to go. We felt we were ready even to die. We knew we could be butchered and our boys might be kidnapped. But we felt peace about going, and in praying with our field director we believed that this particular violent nation was going to open up and the whole nation was going to hear the Gospel.

A Jesuit priest had documented how at that time the government and traditional state church had a plan to destroy all Protestant Christians. Their plan almost succeeded, except—as in Psalm 2—the Lord laughed.

David Had a Dream

The Lord moved in and, with the help of many of that nation's youth, we began to have street meetings and crusades. The young people organized a youth crusade and planned to have a parade right down the main street of the capital city. They carried signs that read, "I believe in Jesus," and "Believe on the Lord Jesus Christ." A local radio station played a record of Gospel songs during the parade and everyone carried a transistor radio so they could sing in unison as they paraded down the main street.

We didn't know if anybody would come or what the police would do. It was a dangerous move. Because I had challenged the young people to do it in the first place, they asked me to be the evangelist for the crusade and I had to walk up in front of the parade. I thought, "Boy, this is a great way to go!" There I was, with a transistor radio, singing "Onward Christian Soldiers" and wondering where the police were going to come from.

We started out with about 7,000, mostly youth, and a few adults. They had come from all over the nation. As we started marching, more and more people joined in. It was a holiday—the Day of the Virgin—so they joined in, many not knowing what our parade was all about.

When we got to the main plaza in the heart of the city, about 20,000 people were there. Later one of my friends told me that I stood on the steps of the capitol building and just laughed. I can't remember doing anything like that, but I believe it! I was so excited that the day I had prayed for, for twelve years, had finally arrived. And the doors had opened in a massive way.

A Man After God's Heart

The president of the republic had an office right on that square. He came out to the edges of the crowd while we were singing, "How Great Thou Art" and he asked a Campus Crusade worker, "What in the world is this?"

"The evangelicals are just singing, Mr. President," he said. "They're going to put a wreath at the feet of the statue of Bolivar. And that fellow up there is going to make a speech."

"My goodness," the president said. "If these evangelicals can gather such a crowd in our capital city, they could get a president into office."

That really shook him. Over the past thirty years that country has some of the fastest-growing evangelical churches in the world. It all started with a vision from God, and the faith and prayers of many Christians—we weren't the only ones—including the faithful missionaries who also were waiting for the Lord to open the doors for decades.

Other things have happened since then. Several years later I stopped in that nation en route from a crusade in Peru to be at three nights of rallies and pastors' conferences. While we were there, we got a call from a former president who is also one of the wealthiest persons in the country. His family was among those that had backed the persecution of evangelical Christians only fifteen to twenty years before. He invited me to his office on the nineteenth floor of a high-rise building. We sat down, had some coffee and chit-chat, and finally got down to business. Our conversation stretched out for more than three hours.

"We fear that the atheists are going to take our land," the man told me. "We have become convinced that the only message ideologically that can stop atheism and keep our families from falling apart is the Gospel that you evangelicals preach." This was coming from someone whose partisans had been behind the persecution against evangelicals not many years before!

As we talked, I explained to him that we'd just held in another country what we called a "Family Festival." At our "Family Festivals" we use television, radio, meetings, rallies, and counseling centers to help families.

"Palau," he said, "if you set up a nationwide Family Festival for our land, we'll foot much of the bill."

Now you might say, "That's a political move." I say, "If they're going to foot the bill, let them make their political moves. Meanwhile, we'll have a chance to preach the Gospel to twenty-five million people." The Lord can do anything. He can move granite mountains. The Lord can do it in our generation!

A few months after this encounter we were invited to be at a Presidential Banquet in that same capital city. The guest list read like a "Who's Who." Besides the president, those attending included three ex-presidents, three presidential candidates, the top military officers, ambassadors from all over the world, and many wealthy people from across the country. I was asked to preach the Gospel for thirty minutes. The president said, "Palau, this message will be on national television." It was.

That was quite a few years ago, but people all over South America continue to hunger for the Gospel. They're coming to Christ, not by ones or twos as before, but by the hundreds and thousands and millions. We've seen the same massive wave of conversions the past decade in Asia and Eastern Europe. It's thrilling!

BE PART OF A MIRACLE

You can take part in a miracle like this. Maybe you think, "Luis, I don't have all the gifts you have. I'm not a public speaker. I don't get around like you do." That's not the point. You don't have to be a powerful speaker, or a visible, public person. Do you walk with God? Do you pray big prayers and dream big dreams?

Any of us, as long as we begin to walk with God like David did, can be used of the Lord to shake up nations for the Gospel. You don't have to be a super-anything. The Lord does amazing things you cannot understand.

David wanted to be used by God to bring his nation back to the Lord. And where did the Lord find him? Out in the pasture—a teenager herding a bunch of sheep. But David had a heart for God, a heart for people, a world-wide vision, and a long-range historical perspective. Even in those Old Testament days, David wanted to be used by God to bring people into a right relationship with Him.

Let me ask you: Do you feel that kind of passion for people to come to Christ? If you don't, what can you do about it? Pray about it. Get on your knees alone or with your spouse and say, "Lord, I want a passion for the lost. Sometimes I couldn't care less, Lord. And I know it's wrong not to care. Give me a love and a passion for people. Not only my neighbors and relatives, but the nations that I don't like at all. Give me a love for the lost."

David Had a Dream

In Psalm 51, David says, "Oh, Lord, cleanse me, forgive me, give me a willing spirit. Then I'll teach transgressors Your way and sinners will be converted to You." The Lord can use anybody who has that kind of heart.

Even if you haven't had all the educational privileges you wish you had—and that would be good to have—the Lord can use you. I don't have all the privileges of education I wish I had and ought to have, but the Lord has seen fit to use me. I believe it's because I really want to be used. And He can do the same with you. The Lord can do mighty things through anyone who is available—man or woman, young or old.

I once told 17,000 Christian university students: "Get yourself a map, either of a nation that is on your heart, or even of the whole world, and begin to pray for nations. Begin to invest time and thought in whole nations. Intercession is spiritual work and by praying in the Holy Spirit you can bind the powers of darkness. Pray until the outline of a nation's map is burned as by fire on your soul" (see Romans 15:30–33).

Through prayer, you can actually stay the hand of Satan (see Daniel 9–10). I believe you can even depose governments by prayer in the Holy Spirit. Few of us have ever learned or practice that. Maybe God will never take you to India or Morocco or Uzbekistan, but He can use you to open up those countries for Jesus Christ and His Gospel through prayer.

I remember when I first visited the United States. I went to a missions conference in Michigan and met a missionary from Pakistan. I got a burden to pray for Pakistan even though my mission and evangelistic work were all in

A Man After God's Heart

Latin America. As I prayed, I figured that some day the Lord would take me to Pakistan and to India to preach the Gospel of Jesus Christ.

About fifteen years later, I started receiving invitations to go on preaching campaigns to several big cities in India. And then, to go to Pakistan.

A few months later in Germany, of all places, one of my greatest joys during a crusade in the city of Essen was meeting a Pakistani fellow by the name of Abdul. He was in Germany studying to be an engineer. During the crusade, Abdul gave his life to the Lord Jesus. I have a picture of him—a very handsome Pakistani. I said to him, "You know, you are the first Pakistani I have ever led to Jesus. For me, this is a fulfillment of prayer. I believe God is going to take me to your country. I've been praying for Pakistan for sixteen years."

He looked at me and said, "Would you repeat that?"

"I've been praying for Pakistan for sixteen years," I said.

"Why would you pray for Pakistan for sixteen years?" He was moved.

"Just because I love you even though I didn't know any of you. I just got this burden from God."

This man began to cry. "Then I'll help you win Pakistan for Christ," he said. He'd been saved for only five minutes and already he had a vision for his country.

Our evangelistic team has seen thousands of Abduls converted to Christ in India and Pakistan in recent years.

The Lord can do miraculous things with our lives. We have to allow Him room to work. Our problem is this:

Instead of presenting ourselves as those "alive from the dead" we waste time with our television sets and our trite jokes and our little holidays and we don't get the big picture. We mouth the words and say we're available to be used of God—but how could He get through to us if He actually wanted to use us?

Perhaps you remember when David Wilkerson first sensed God's call to minister to the hardened gang members in the back streets of New York. The gang ministry came about after he decided to sell his television set and use the hours he normally watched TV as a special nightly prayer time before God. One night while he was on his knees in the former TV room, the Lord challenged him with this great ministry opportunity. What am I saying—that everyone should go out and sell their television sets? That's not the point.

The question is: How open are you to the voice of God? How willing are you to pray and agonize over lost individuals outside of your own little circle of friends and family? How ready are you to start where you are and plunge into the work of touching lives for Christ in your own neighborhood in your own small way?

That's what King David had to do. He started as a teenager. When he got to be thirty, he took a segment of the kingdom. Finally, when he was thirty-seven, he took over the entire nation. The Lord gave him a name and success wherever he turned.

Do you have a worldwide vision? A long-range historical perspective? Do you see the nations with God's eyes when you read the newspaper, *Time, Newsweek*, and *U. S. News and World Report*? Do you look at unfolding world events and say, "What is my Father trying to do? What's He doing in China? In Iran? In Mali? In the Ukraine?"

You've got to get involved in the spiritual battle in the heavenly places. Read Ephesians 6:10–20. God can answer the prayers of some relatively unknown person and open up nations to Himself and for His glory. He did it through David. He's doing it today. He will do it through you. He wills to do so—do you?

Chapter 8

A Sharp and Ready Arrow

IF DAVID HAD the type of tombstone on which they chisel an epitaph in the granite, what was said of him in Acts 13:36 would have served well:

> FOR WHEN DAVID HAD SERVED GOD'S PURPOSE IN
> HIS OWN GENERATION, HE FELL ASLEEP; HE WAS
> BURIED WITH HIS FATHERS AND HIS BODY DECAYED.

David served the purpose of God and he served his own generation. He died. He was buried.

And so it goes. People are born, live, die, and then their bodies decay. Many people brought up in the Western culture don't like to be around death. They can hardly wait for the mortuary to come and take away the body. These days, people usually die in hospitals, shut away from their families, and especially the children.

I was ten years old when my father died. They wanted to keep me away from the cemetery and burial ceremony, but I really wanted to go. So I jumped out the kitchen window and hid in the truck that went to the cemetery. Standing a little distance away, I watched them put the body of my father into the earth. It was a traumatic experience, but also one of the healthiest experiences of my life.

I knew my father died singing a hymn. He knew he was going to be with the Lord Jesus after he died. After all, to be absent from the body is to be present with the Lord, the inerrant Word of God assures us in 2 Corinthians 5:8. As I watched his body being put into the grave, I remembered how I'd been told that someday his body would be raised. Standing there alone in the cemetery, I believed it. It hurt a lot to know that I wouldn't see Dad for the rest of my life, but I knew he was better off than I was.

I'm glad I saw my dad buried. Even at that young age, it made me think very soberly about life. After that day, I knew that death was real, not just something that happens in the movies. I knew that it happened to real people . . . to people whom you have loved.

A REASON TO LIVE

Death happens all the time. You too will die unless the Lord returns first (1 Thessalonians 4). Maybe you're one of these persons who coasts along signing checks, shaving, bathing, eating, buying, selling, raising children, paying off the mortgage, and saying that's it—that's all there is. But is that really life? No. There's more than that. For those of us who are looking forward to being with Jesus Christ, life has a purpose.

David's life had a purpose; Acts 13:36 says so. His purpose was the purpose of God—"in his own generation." We can scream all we want about the mistakes of the past generation. We can dream and project ourselves all we want concerning the future generation. But there's nothing much we can do about either one. We can, however, have a dynamic effect on our own generation. We've only one generation to live in. Certainly, we may modify little bits of the past generation's actions. We will definitely influence some of the future ones. But God holds us accountable for what we do in *our* generation. In that light we discern our purpose.

It's a beautiful thought. Most people, at least those who have at least half their wits about them, actually want to live profitable, truthful, productive lives. Only an absolute moron would want to just drift through life, pick up his paycheck, go on a holiday, get another paycheck, go on another holiday, and succumb to the illusion that this is all there is to life.

Many people outside the Body of Christ live this way, but I can't imagine any true believer willing to just float down the river of life like an empty raft, ending up in the ocean or smashed to pieces on the rocks. It's so much better to serve God's purpose with our lives in our generation. And there is a purpose for each of us.

WEAPONS OF RIGHTEOUSNESS

There's a verse in Romans that doesn't even mention the name of David but speaks with authority as to the way he lived.

> *Do not offer the parts of your body to sin, as instruments of wickedness, but rather offer your-*

A Man After God's Heart

selves to God, as those who have been brought
from death to life; and offer the parts of your body
to him as instruments of righteousness
(Romans 6:13).

Another way to translate *instruments* is "weapons." Then
the verse would read: "Offer the parts of your body to him as
weapons of righteousness." Isn't that powerful? That means I
can actually pick myself up, so to speak, and present myself
to God by saying, "Lord, I present my members to You, to be
weapons of righteousness for You." To think that my eyes, my
hands, my mouth, my mind, my emotions, my will—all can
be weapons for God. What a motivating thought!

What about you? Are you a weapon of righteousness
or unrighteousness? There is no middle ground. You can't
say, "Oh well, on Sundays I am a weapon of righteousness, but the rest of the week I can coast a little bit, you
know."

From his earliest years David wanted to be a powerful
weapon in the hand of his God. And isn't it much better to
decide to serve God from your youth? The holier you are
from the earliest possible age, the more powerful a weapon
in the hands of God you will be. God can use anybody. In
fact, one time He decided to use a donkey. But God prefers
to use holy, totally yielded people.

One of John Wesley's followers was Robert Murray
M'Cheyne, a very powerful young man who died when he
was only twenty-nine years old. I have copied in the front
of my Bible a portion of a letter he wrote to a man named
Mr. Edwards. It reads: "Mr. Edwards, according to your

144

holiness, so shall be your success. A holy man is an awesome weapon in the hands of God."

An awesome weapon! Now, most of us would say we're anything but awesome. Nevertheless, we *can* be as God uses us, and Scripture supports the idea. How our Lord longs to hear us pray, "Dear God, here am I. Here are my members. Lord, I present them to You. Make them weapons of righteousness."

There's no telling what He will do with a life so yielded to His purposes. He can use you with mighty power, He may take you anywhere in the world, He may choose to do as He pleases, but you can count on one thing—He will turn you and your members into weapons of righteousness. Why don't you, right now, make a definite decision, based on Romans 12:1–2? Man or woman, whatever your age. The sooner you do it, the better. That way you'll avoid accumulating the scars, the bitter memories, and the haunting regrets of a life lived away from God. That's why I'm committed to youth crusades and meetings where the students and workers can dedicate their young, unscarred lives to God's purposes. They may not understand all that will come in the wake of that decision, but God will take them at their word, if they mean business, and He will really begin to use them.

NOT ABILITY, BUT AVAILABILITY

Perhaps you believe you aren't clever, educated, or beautiful enough for the Lord to use you. My mind goes back to a situation at one of our crusades in Paraguay, South America, many years ago.

A Man After God's Heart

Over the years, we have often set up family counseling centers where people can come for spiritual help. One of our team members, Dr. James M. Williams, has been in charge of setting up these centers and training local people to work in them. It is his usual practice to recruit pastors or professional people to work in the centers, people with a postgraduate education. Jim Williams looks for counselors who are trained not only in how to lead people to Christ but also in how to deal with deeper family problems, such as divorce, adultery, homosexuality, and so on.

At this particular crusade in Paraguay we had as many as seventy people at one time waiting at these family counseling centers for help. Since only about thirty-five had been trained to counsel, that meant not everybody could be helped at once.

As director, Jim got kind of nervous about that, especially since one of the people who took the counseling course was a "nonprofessional." This one man—we'll call him José—couldn't even read or write. But he loved the Lord and had a fantastic memory. He came to the counseling classes and when exam time came he knew all the answers because he had memorized them as the class went along! But because José couldn't read or write, Jim asked the receptionist not to assign any cases to José unless they were really minor ones—because José might seriously misdirect the counselee.

One day all the counselors were busy and in came a very sharp-looking gentleman. He was obviously a white-collar individual, upper middle-class. The only one left without a person to counsel was illiterate José. The secretary got flustered. José was alert, however, and walked right up and said, "I'll counsel with this gentleman." The secretary was too bashful and embarrassed to say, "No, José, let's call our supervisor, Mr. Williams."

So José sat down with this gentleman, talked with him, and led him to Jesus Christ. The fellow turned out to be a medical doctor. Meanwhile, the secretary had gotten through to Jim and explained the situation.

When the doctor and José came out after counseling, Jim over-eagerly greeted the doctor but just got a quick, perfunctory "Hello" in reply. Jim thought, "José must have really ruined that one." So Jim told the secretary, "Next time some distinguished-looking person like this comes in for counseling, make sure he goes to someone else. Don't give him to José. If I'm busy, come and call me anyway and I will take care of it."

The next day the same doctor returned, but this time he was accompanied by two men. These men were well-dressed and sharp-looking, apparently important people, too. The center was again extremely busy—except for this one illiterate brother who was sitting without anything to do. The secretary dashed off to get Jim and he hurried in and turned on the charm, "Oh, DOC-tor! How ARE you!"

The doctor said, "I want my two friends here to meet the gentleman who talked to me yesterday and helped me to receive Jesus Christ.

Jim said, "I'll be glad to take care of you."

"No," said the doctor, "I want José to talk to them."

So they had to get this illiterate brother and bring him

in. Nobody knows what José said because the doctor wanted to be alone with him and his friends. But José led these other two men—who were also doctors—to faith in Jesus Christ. And the next day, to top it off, the three doctors got together and brought another friend who was having family problems. And this same illiterate brother led the fourth man to Christ.

The following week, the doctors had a party and the only one of the counseling staff they invited was humble, uneducated José.

Most of us would have responded as Jim did. We would have looked at José and thought, "This man is so incapable." He even needed his twelve-year-old nephew to help him fill out the decision cards. After he counseled, the little boy had to do the writing. But in three days the Lord used him to lead four doctors to Jesus. Who you are makes no difference to God, if you're available to Jesus Christ.

If a humble brother like José could be used of the Lord to win sophisticated, professional people to Christ— and they loved him so much they threw a party for him— listen, what could He do through you if you were surrendered to Him? What could He accomplish if you would say to Him, "Lord, I present You my body as a weapon for righteousness"?

That's what David did, and David served his own generation by the will of God. Then he fell asleep and he saw corruption. In other words, he died. That was the end of David. Someday that will be the end of us, too. When we die, the question will be: "Did you choose to serve the purpose of God in this generation, or did you choose to float along like a dead fish downstream?" The choice is yours.

BIG DOORS, SMALL HINGES

If you are a believer, the Lord surely has something for you to do. Something, perhaps, that will exceed your wildest imaginations. He'll do the abundant thing in your life, more than you could ever ask or think.

I was born and grew up in Argentina. I was a South American. I had no connections. I was the son of a widow and had to help support her financially. There was no chance, from a human standpoint, that my dreams of becoming an evangelist to masses of people across a continent would be fulfilled.

But one day the Lord sent to our city two Americans I'd never heard of before. One was Dr. Dick Hillis and the other Dr. Ray Stedman. I was twenty-two then. Because I'd been to British boarding schools and knew English, I went to hear them. I went mostly out of curiosity, but something seemed to pull me in.

After the meetings I went up to talk with these two Americans. Because of that simple encounter that lasted only thirty-six hours, the Lord opened vast doors to His glory. He soon moved me out of Argentina and took me to what is now Multnomah Biblical Seminary in Portland, Oregon. There I met my wife, Patricia. The doors opened, and more and more things began to happen.

I couldn't foresee any of that. I didn't twist God's arm or people's arms. I just waited for His timing. And you can do it, too. Psalm 37:3–5 belongs to all of us. That doesn't mean that some day you'll be preaching to presidents. The Lord may well have something better than that for you. There is an old saying I wish was in the Bible: "Big doors turn on small hinges."

When I went to that little meeting where Hillis and Stedman were speaking, I had absolutely no idea my life would be thrust in a new, exciting direction beginning that very day. I simply went to that service because I felt an urge to do so, and now I see the Lord wanted me to. I might have stayed home and read a book or gone for a walk instead. How different my life would have been!

When Jesse sent the picnic lunch to his sons at the battle line, David might well have said, "Why should I risk my neck taking sandwiches to my brothers? Let them eat Army rations. I'm going back to my flocks." Then David might have never met Goliath . . . nor his destiny.

Maybe you're waiting for the big break. And the big break never seems to come. One old saying has been knocked around in the world for a long time: "It took me twenty years to become an overnight success." In other words, the outworking of God's purpose doesn't necessarily happen overnight.

TRUST HIS TIMING

God simply wants you to be surrendered and available to Him, wherever He's placed you. Let Him make you into a powerful weapon of righteousness. If God decides to leave you in His quiver for a while instead of launching you at some great target—that's all right. Don't

worry about it. He knows His business. You just concen-
trate on being His sharp and ready arrow—available for
His timing and for His glory.

> *Wait for the LORD;*
>> *be strong and take heart*
>> *and wait for the LORD* (Psalm 27:14).

Take that from someone who knows—David himself.
Waiting for the Lord is the deepest proof of a heart after God.

Recommended Reading

To further enrich your Christian life, look for the following books in your local Christian bookstore. If the store doesn't have one of these books in stock, ask the sales clerk to order it for you.

ADVENTURING THROUGH THE BIBLE by Ray C. Stedman (Discovery House Publishers)

AUTHENTIC CHRISTIANITY by Ray C. Stedman (Discovery House Publishers)

BODY LIFE by Ray C. Stedman (Discovery House Publishers)

CALLING AMERICA AND THE NATIONS TO CHRIST by Luis Palau (Thomas Nelson Publishers)

GOD IS RELEVANT by Luis Palau (Doubleday)

HEALTHY HABITS FOR SPIRITUAL GROWTH by Luis Palau (Discovery House Publishers)

A LIFE OF INTEGRITY by Howard Hendricks, general editor (Multnomah Books)

LUIS PALAU by W. Terry Whalin (Bethany House Publishers)

MORE THAN CONQUERORS by John Woodbridge, general editor (Moody Press)

THE ONLY HOPE FOR AMERICA by Luis Palau (Crossway Books)

THE PETER PROMISE by Luis Palau (Discovery House Publishers)

SAY YES! HOW TO RENEW YOUR SPIRITUAL PASSION by Luis Palau (Discovery House Publishers)

SEVEN PROMISES OF A PROMISE KEEPER by Luis Palau, et al. (Focus on the Family Publishing)

SHARING CHRIST WHEN YOU FEEL YOU CAN'T by Daniel Owens (Crossway Books)

YOUR NEW LIFE WITH CHRIST by Luis Palau (Crossway Books)

About the Author

Who is Luis Palau? Perhaps you've followed his ministry with interest for years. Or perhaps this book is your first introduction to the man.

Luis Palau is now becoming well known in his adopted homeland, America. His popularity in Latin America, the United Kingdom, and other parts of the world is rather remarkable.

During one crusade, more than 518,000 people in London turned out to hear Luis Palau in person. And a crowd of 700,000 people gathered to hear Luis on Thanksgiving Sunday in Guatemala a few years ago.

In many ways, Luis Palau stands out in this generation as a truly international Christian spokesman and leader. He's a third generation transplanted European who grew up in the province of Buenos Aires, Argentina, and then chose to become an American citizen after completing the graduate course at Multnomah Biblical Seminary in Portland, Oregon.

Equally at ease in English and Spanish, Luis Palau's solidly biblical, practical messages hit home in the minds and hearts of listeners around the world.

"Luis is probably more in demand among evangelicals to preach and speak than almost any other person in the world," says Billy Graham. "Wherever there is an evangelical conference they try to get Luis Palau, because he is a powerful preacher. But more than that, he is an evangelist to whom God has given a multiplicity of gifts."

Luis Palau has proclaimed the Good News of Jesus Christ to hundreds of millions of people via radio and television in ninety-five countries, and face-to-face to more than twelve million people on six continents.

The impact? Many hundreds of thousands of people have trusted Jesus Christ and become established as disciples in local churches. Cities and nations have heard a clear-cut proclamation of the Gospel. Luis Palau's burden is to see the same thing happen in America, in this generation.

Luis and his wife, Pat, also a popular conference speaker and author, have served as missionary-evangelists in Costa Rica, Colombia, and Mexico. The Palaus have four grown sons and now make their home in Portland, Oregon, near the international headquarters of the Luis Palau Evangelistic Association.

Correspondence

If this book has motivated you to have a heart after God, or if you have been helped in any other way through the varied ministries of the Luis Palau Evangelistic Association, please let me know. I'd love to hear from you! My address is:

Luis Palau
P.O. Box 1173
Portland, OR 97207, U.S.A.
lpea@palau.org
http://www.gospelcom.net/lpea

Note to the Reader